SEVEN D[AYS]
In Dirty Water
50 FUN DEVOTIONS FOR KIDS

Mary Rose Pearson

TYNDALE
KIDS

Tyndale House Publishers, Inc.
Wheaton, Illinois

Visit Tyndale's exciting Web site at www.tyndale.com

Edited by Betty Free
Designed by Jenny Destree

ISBN 0-8423-3794-6

Printed in the United States of America

07 06 05 04 03 02 01 00
8   7   6   5   4   3   2   1

To my husband, Evangelist M. N. Pearson,
whose help, support, and encouragement
are invaluable to my writing,
and whose love makes my life rich and complete.

To our three children, twelve grandchildren,
and five great-grandchildren,
to whom we will pass the torch someday.
Ever hold it high!

CONTENTS

INTRODUCTION

This is a book of facts, Bible stories, and learning activities for children to read and enjoy for themselves, for parents to use in home devotions, or for teachers to employ in any number of church settings. It can also be used in church or home schools. *Please note,* church leaders and teachers, that Tyndale House gives you permission to photocopy the puzzles for use in church school, kids' groups, and so on.

The Bible contains a treasury of exciting adventure stories. Through them, we learn how God worked in the lives of ordinary people like ourselves. Those people and their stories show us the blessings and benefits of trusting and obeying God along with the troubles that come from disobeying him.

The purpose of this book is to inspire children to love and appreciate God's Book more, to increase their knowledge of it, and to live by its precepts. Each devotion includes a "This Is for You" section in which children can see how they may apply Bible truths to their own lives.

Learning certain facts can help us understand stories from Bible times better. For this reason, kids will find important information about objects, places, people, or customs that are a part of the story. The short, interesting facts make the stories come alive and have more meaning. The learning activities are fun and challenging. They reinforce the Bible stories and the personal applications.

All the material is new in this book, which is a companion to the popular *Frogs in Pharaoh's Bed*. This book differs in one way: The stories are in chronological order, so the reader can get a sense of continuity from Adam and Eve to the Rapture. The Bible stories may be used in any order desired, however.

May our Lord use this book to increase your love for the Lord and for the Grand Old Book that is timeless in meeting the needs of today.

1

Enticing Fruit and a Sneaky Snake

Introduction

Watch and pray so that you will not fall into temptation. The spirit is willing, but the body is weak.

Mark 14:38

Snake! Snake!" Megan yelled as she frantically swam to her friends. Gasping for breath, she cried, "There's a cottonmouth moccasin in the boathouse. I almost put my hand on him before I saw him. Let's get out of the water fast!" The girls scrambled to shore and ran far away from the deadly snake.

In the Garden of Eden, Eve came "eyeball to eyeball" with a snake one day. Because she didn't run away, the snake did something to her that was far worse than giving her a poisonous bite.

THE FACTS, PLEASE!

1. *Species of snakes.* About 2500 species of snakes are known. Only eight out of 100 are poisonous.
2. *A snake's body.* The long, flexible body of a snake contains a large number of vertebrae; some snakes have as many as 300. Each vertebra, after the first two, has a pair of slender ribs. This light skeletal structure makes it easy for the snake to coil, to swim, and to glide along rapidly without legs.
3. *Why don't snakes have legs?* Why do they crawl on the ground? Apparently, the snake once walked upright and was the most beautiful, intelligent animal in the Garden of Eden. Our Bible story tells us why God changed snakes into hated, crawling reptiles.
4. *Two special trees.* These grew in the middle of the Garden of Eden. One was "the tree of the knowledge of good and evil" (Genesis 2:9). What fruit did it have? Apples? Pears? Watermelon? No. There is no fruit today like the fruit on that tree.

Bible Story: Help Yourself, Eve
Genesis 3

A snake sneaked through the Garden of Eden one day. He was looking for the woman God had made. This crafty, beautiful creature planned to trick Eve into sinning. Why would a snake care if Eve sinned? The answer: He was really Satan in disguise. Maybe he found Eve near the tree of the knowledge of good and evil. Or maybe he lured her there.

The sneaky snake slyly argued that Eve should eat the enticing fruit. "You will be like God, knowing good and evil," he said. Eve saw that the fruit was good for food. It looked delicious, and she wanted to be wise like God.

Eve took some fruit and ate it. Worse yet, Adam also ate some when she offered it to him. Satan must have been very pleased, thinking, *Yippee! They sinned—just as I planned!*

Adam and Eve had never known evil before. Now they were ashamed, because they realized they were naked. Even the aprons they made from fig leaves didn't cover them well. When they heard the sound of God's voice in the garden, they hid behind some trees.

Of course God saw them. He told Eve, "You will have pain in childbearing."

God said to Adam, "The ground will be cursed, and you will have to work hard to make a living."

Because the snake let Satan use him, God said, "You will crawl on your belly and eat dust." Ever since that day, snakes have had no legs, and they move by slithering over the ground.

This Is for You

God also named another punishment for Satan. He promised that someone would come to crush the serpent's head (meaning Satan). Years later, the Promised One (the Lord Jesus) came. He defeated Satan when he died on the cross for the sins of the whole world.

When we were born, we inherited a sin nature from Adam. Because of it, we want to sin. We are on Satan's side, listening to his temptations and sinning. This makes Satan happy.

're still on Satan's side, you can move over to God's side! Turn from sin and believe in Jesus as your Savior. He will forgive all your sins, and you will be born into God's family. Would you like to ask Jesus to save you? *See the last page of this book.* Remember, God is more powerful than that sneaky snake, Satan!

Word Search:
Trouble in the Garden

Find and circle the following words, which are found in this devotion. You may go up, down, across, backward, or diagonally. Some words share letters.

ADAM	EDEN	FRUIT	LEGS	SNEAKY
ATE	ENTICING	GARDEN	NAKED	TEMPTATION
BELIEVE	EVE	GLIDE	POISONOUS	TREES
BELLY	EVIL	GOD	SATAN	WANT
CRAWL	FAMILY	GOOD	SAVIOR	WISE
CROSS	FOOD	HELP	SIN	
DIED	FORGIVE	KNOWLEDGE	SNAKE	

4

```
W  P  L  E  H  S  A  T  A  N  U  Y  T
R  T  N  A  W  H  Y  W  I  S  E  N  R
S  S  G  O  D  L  B  E  L  I  E  V  E
K  G  P  O  I  S  O  N  O  U  S  E  E
N  E  N  M  O  T  A  D  A  M  N  D  S
O  L  A  C  F  D  A  V  B  T  S  I  N
W  F  K  R  R  A  E  T  I  E  E  L  E
L  T  E  A  U  V  E  C  P  O  L  G  A
E  S  D  W  I  D  I  E  D  M  R  L  K
D  T  O  L  T  N  G  A  R  D  E  N  Y
G  F  O  R  G  I  V  E  D  E  N  T  N
E  D  F  C  C  R  O  S  S  N  A  K  E
```

2

No Blood
in an Apple

Introduction

**By faith Abel offered God a better sacrifice than Cain
did. By faith he was commended as a righteous man,
when God spoke well of his offerings. And by faith he
still speaks, even though he is dead.**

Hebrews 11:4

OUCH! You prick your finger, and some red, sticky stuff
oozes out. What is it? It's your blood, of course. It is a very
important part of your body. You can't live without it.

On a rural highway, two cars crash head-on. One driver,
who is badly hurt, is bleeding profusely. Other motorists
stop, call 9-1-1, and give what first aid they can. When an
ambulance arrives, a medic calls for a helicopter to transport
the injured man to the hospital. "This man has lost a lot of
blood," the medic says. "This man must have a transfusion
immediately."

The Facts, Please

1. *The importance of blood.* Every part of our body depends on blood for food. Our bloodstream not only carries nourishment and oxygen to our tissues, but takes away waste products and carbon dioxide. Blood moves through our body so quickly that all of it passes through our heart every two or three minutes.

2. *The flow of blood.* It is important for blood to flow to every part of our body. If it is shut off from one part for an hour, that part may die. If it is shut off from the brain, the person will black out and soon die. If someone's body loses one-third of its blood suddenly, that person will die.

3. *Life in blood.* God said, "The life of a creature is in the blood" (Leviticus 17:11). Our lives depend on our blood.

4. *Our eternal life.* This depends on blood, too. From the first, God taught people to sacrifice an animal when they disobeyed him. They had to shed the animal's blood to make up for their sins. Those animal sacrifices have now been replaced by Jesus' one-time sacrifice for our sins, when he shed his blood on the cross. If we believe in him, he gives us eternal life.

Bible Story: A Bloody Lamb Beats the Fruit
Genesis 4:1-16

Waaa, waaa! It is the cry of the first baby in the world. Awesome! That's how Adam and Eve must have felt when they saw him. They named their son Cain. Soon Cain had a brother, Abel. These two boys inherited sin natures from their parents, which means it was natural for them to sin by disobeying God.

When Cain and Abel were grown, they had to work to make a living. Cain chose to be a farmer. He planted a garden and raised crops, such as grains and fruit. Abel became a shepherd.

One day Cain and Abel each brought an offering to God. Their parents must have taught them about God and how they were to worship him by shedding the blood of an animal.

Cain brought an offering of something he had grown—maybe a basket of fruit or some grain. It did not have a drop of blood in it. Abel killed a lamb by shedding its blood. His offering showed he knew he had sinned and wanted God to forgive him.

God was pleased with Abel's offering, but not Cain's. This made Cain very angry. "Why are you angry?" God asked him. "You can still bring the right offering." Did Cain do it? Oh, no! Instead, he killed his brother and buried him in the ground.

That was the end of Abel on this earth. It was not the end of Abel forever, though. Because he believed God and followed his instructions, Abel's sins were forgiven. We will see him in heaven someday.

This Is for You

We, too, are guilty of sin, just as Cain and Abel were. But we don't need to kill a lamb and shed its blood to have our sins forgiven. A bloody lamb in the Old Testament was a picture of Jesus, the Lamb of God. He came to earth and died on the cross, shedding his blood for us. Ever since then, God forgives people's sins when they believe in his Son, Jesus, as Savior.

Cain brought an offering that did not please God. It was not a picture of Jesus, because Cain did not shed an animal's blood for his offering.

Many people think their good deeds, their baptism, or their church membership will save them. What's wrong? No blood. They have turned their back on the Savior who died for them.

Do you ever thank Jesus for dying for you? Have you received him as your Savior? *See the last page of this book.*

Fill in the Blanks in the Verses:
Nothing but the Blood

1. What's Missing?

On the blank line, print the letter that's missing from the second word in each set of words below.

In LAMBS	but not in	SLAM	___
In SLAW	but not in	WAS	___
In NOTE	but not in	TEN	___
In BOAT	but not in	TAB	___
In CRADLE	but not in	CLEAR	___

Reading down, what word have you written on the lines above? _____

2. Coded Words

Write the word from the first section of this puzzle on all the blank lines in the verses below that have the number *1* underneath them. Then, using the code, fill in the remaining blanks in the verses.

	1	2	3	4
a	I	S	D	R
b	G	O	P	U
c	F	E	N	V

1. "Without the shedding of _____ there is no
    1

___ ___ ___ ___ ___ ___ ___ ___ ___ ___ ___." (Hebrews 9:22)
c-1 b-2 a-4 b-1 a-1 c-4 c-2 c-3 c-2 a-2 a-2

2. "To him who loves us and has ___ ___ ___ ___ ___ us from
                                c-1 a-4 c-2 c-2 a-3
our sins by his _____." (Revelation 1:5)
                    1

3. "The _____ of Jesus, his Son,
        1

___ ___ ___ ___ ___ ___ ___ ___ us from all sin." (1 John 1:7)
b-3 b-4 a-4 a-1 c-1 a-1 c-2 a-2

11

3

Big-City Life or a Nomad's Tent

Introduction

By faith Abraham, when called to go to a place he would later receive as his inheritance, obeyed and went, even though he did not know where he was going.

Hebrews 11:8

WHY? Why do I have to do that?" Sound familiar? Maybe you have said those words a few times to your parents.

"Hey, Josh, I've got one!" Jeremy yelled as he pulled a fish into the boat.

"And I have a nibble," said Josh. "Maybe we've finally found a good fishing spot."

Then they heard their father call, "Hurry home, boys. A bad storm is coming!"

"What's he talking about? There's hardly a cloud in the sky," Jeremy grumbled. "Why do we have to go home just when the fishing is getting good?"

"I don't know, but I guess we'd better obey Dad," replied Josh, beginning to row the boat toward shore. Soon a brisk wind began to blow and rain spattered down. The boys beached their boat and ran for home just before a furious storm broke.

"Wow! It's a good thing we obeyed Dad right away," exclaimed Jeremy. "I'd hate to be out in that boat now."

THE FACTS, PLEASE!

1. *Birth of Abraham.* He was born about 4000 years ago in Ur, one of the largest, most progressive cities of the ancient world. It stood on the banks of the Euphrates River, high on an artificial plateau. Inside its huge walls lived a splendid civilization of a quarter million or more people.
2. *Ur.* When archaeologists dug down to this once-great city, they found the remains of fine houses, libraries, and temples. Clay tablets revealed that people learned mathematics, language, geography, botany, and drawing in their schools.
3. *The people of Ur.* They worshiped Nanna, the moon god, and many other gods. In the center of Ur stood a huge ziggurat (a system of terraced platforms). Nanna's temple was on top.
4. *Tents in Abraham's time.* These were covered with cloth from goat hair or skin or from camel skin, sewn together in one long piece. The tent dweller stretched this cloth over poles, made it taut, and fastened it to stakes in the ground.

Bible Story: He Didn't Know Where He Was Going
Genesis 11:26–12:9; 21:1-5; 22:17-18

Let's visit the city of Ur. The year is about 2000 B.C. Here we see great crowds of people jostling one another in the narrow streets, heading for the moon god's temple. Priests will offer a human sacrifice to Nanna there. Other people bring offerings to small idols on side streets or worship a family idol at home. Only Abraham worships the real God.

One day God said to Abraham, "Leave your country and your people, and go to a land that I will show you. I will bless you there."

Abraham did not ask why. He did not complain about leaving the comforts and pleasures of a big city. He obeyed God and went. He took with him his wife, some other relatives, and a big caravan of servants. He also took flocks of sheep and goats, as well as herds of cattle. Where were they going? They didn't know, but God did.

They traveled many miles northwest to Haran, where they stayed until Abraham's father died. Then Abraham's caravan traveled southwest, toward Canaan. On and on they went, up hills and down, over dry, hot countryside.

In the land of Canaan, Abraham lived in tents. Wherever he stopped, he set up an altar and worshiped God. "I will give this land to you and your family," God promised him.

When Abraham was 100 years old, God gave him a son, Isaac. Abraham continued to worship and obey God. Then God promised, "I will bless you and give you a big family. It

15

will be as big as the number of stars in the sky and the grains of sand on the seashore." The Jews, God's special nation of Israel, are Abraham's descendants. Today the total number of Jews worldwide is about 13.5 million. Over 4.5 million live in Israel, the land God gave to Abraham.

This Is for You

To be saved we must receive Jesus as our Savior and Lord. But he does not become Lord of our life unless we obey him. If we let him be Lord, we will follow his plan for us. He will always lead us in the right way, even if we don't know where we're headed.

A freight car carries things from one place to another, but it can't do this all by itself. A train engine pulls the car and it follows, going wherever the engine takes it.

As God's children we are like freight cars, and the engine reminds us of Jesus. We can't do what we should all by ourselves. If we let Jesus be in charge, though, we'll be on the right track. Our "freight car" will be loaded with blessings. And when we arrive in heaven, we'll be very glad we obeyed.

Coded Message:
For What City Was Abraham Looking?

The Bible says Abraham left the big city of Ur because "he was looking forward to the city with foundations, whose architect and builder is God" (Hebrews 11:10). To find what city that is, write the letter on the blank line that follows the letter given (Note that *A* follows *Z*). Then read down from the arrows.

1. God promised Abraham an

⬇

__ __ __ __ __ __ __ __ __ __ __ in the place
H M G D Q H S Z M B D

where he was going.

⬇

2. Abraham __ __ __ __ __ __ God and went, making his
N A D X D C

⬇

home in the promised land by __ __ __ __ __.
E Z H S G

⬇ ⬇

3. Abraham __ __ __ __ __ in __ __ __ __ __
K H U D C S D M S R

⬇

like a __ __ __ __ __ __ __ __ in a foreign country.
R S Q Z M F D Q

Abraham looked forward to going to _____.
Read Hebrews 11:8-10.

From a Pit to a Palace

Introduction

I am your brother Joseph, the one you sold into Egypt! And now, do not be distressed and do not be angry with yourselves for selling me here, because it was to save lives that God sent me ahead of you.

Genesis 45:4-5

CLANG! A door slams shut behind a prisoner who stumbles into a damp, dark prison. Is this a criminal paying for his wicked deeds? No. It is John Bunyan, who has been arrested for preaching without a license in England in the 1600s.

For 12 years John Bunyan endured miserable conditions in his prison. After his release he went back to preaching. Again he was arrested. During that prison stay he wrote *Pilgrim's Progress*, perhaps the most widely read book next to the Bible. It has blessed many generations of people.

John Bunyan could have said, "I was faithful to God.

Why did he let this happen?" But he didn't. Before he went to court he prayed for God's will to be done. Later he said, "I did meet my God sweetly in the prison."

The Facts, Please!

1. *A coat of many colors.* In Bible times almost everyone wore a tunic coat, which was something like a sack. It had a V-shaped opening for the head, with slits for the arms. Usually, it had sleeves. Sometimes men's tunics had brightly-colored stripes woven into the cloth.
2. *A cistern.* A cistern is a pit dug in the dirt or in rock for collection and storage of rain water. In the long dry season in Bible times, a cistern was often dry.
3. *A caravan.* A caravan consisted of a group of people who traveled together, especially in desert regions. Merchants often journeyed like that, using pack animals such as donkeys and camels to carry themselves and the items they were selling or trading.
4. *Prisons and palaces.* Prisons in Old Testament times were often natural pits or dungeons. In Egypt, Joseph was living in the house of the captain of the guard when he was put in the king's prison. Palaces were the homes of important officials.

Bible Story: The Pet in the Pit
Genesis 37:1-4, 12-36; 39; 41

"Go and see how your brothers and our flocks of sheep are doing," Jacob said. Seventeen-year-old Joseph put on his splendid tunic coat of many colors and started out. He wore the coat proudly, knowing his father had given it to him because he loved him more than any of his brothers.

Joseph's brothers were jealous of him because of the coat. They had become even more jealous when Joseph told them he dreamed he would rule over them one day. Now when Joseph arrived, the brothers stripped off his beautiful coat and threw him into a cistern. Soon a caravan of merchants came toward them on their way to Egypt, their camels loaded with spices.

The brothers hauled Joseph out of the pit and sold him to the merchants. In Egypt the merchants sold Joseph as a slave to Potiphar, one of Pharaoh's officials. Joseph did good work, and Potiphar made Joseph the ruler over his house. But after his wife told lies about Joseph, Potiphar put Joseph in prison.

When Joseph was 30 years old, God worked a miracle. He showed Joseph the meaning of two mysterious dreams that Pharaoh had. Joseph told Pharaoh there would be seven years when plenty of crops would grow, and then seven years of a bad famine when no crops would grow. He gave Pharaoh a plan for saving food.

Pharaoh took Joseph out of prison and put him in his palace as the ruler next in importance to him. Joseph's plan worked, and people had food during the famine. Best of all, Joseph's brothers came to Egypt for food. He told them who he was and forgave them for what they had done to him. Jacob and all his family moved to Egypt, and Joseph enjoyed a loving relationship with his father once more.

This Is For You

In spite of his troubles, Joseph worked faithfully on the job, and he obeyed God. At last he saw why God had allowed his problems. It was to save lives, even those of his own family.

When troubles come, it is right to check how we've been living and to pray that God will make us aware of any sins we need to confess to him. If we have been obedient to God, we can be satisfied that he has a reason for allowing trouble to come. He says in Romans 8:28, "We know that in all things God works for the good of those who love him, who have been called according to his purpose."

Neither John Bunyan nor Joseph knew right away how God was bringing good out of trouble. It's the same for us when things go wrong. Has God promised that in all things he works for the good of his children? Yes! Does he keep his promises? Always.

When bad things happen, trust God. Confess your sins. Then be a faithful, obedient Christian. Someday, either on this earth or in heaven, you will see as Joseph did that God has worked all things for your good. Perhaps God will have worked things out for the good of many others, too.

Match-up:
When Good Comes from Bad

Draw a line from each sentence's beginning to its ending.

1. Joseph's father gave him a coat of many   cistern.

2. Joseph's brothers were   Egypt.

3. They put him in a   husband.

4. Then they sold him to some   trusted.

5. Joseph ended up in Egypt as a   colors.

6. Potiphar's wife lied about Joseph to her   jealous.

7. Potiphar put Joseph in   famine.

8. People always found Joseph could be   good.

9. Joseph told Pharaoh the meaning of his   ruler.

10. Joseph advised Pharaoh about the coming   merchants.

11. Pharaoh made Joseph an important   starving.

12. Joseph saved many people from   prison.

13. Joseph's family all moved to   slave.

14. God worked all things in Joseph's life for   dreams.

5

Mud-and-Straw Bricks

Introduction

I am the Lord, and I will bring you out from under the yoke of the Egyptians. I will free you from being slaves to them, and I will redeem you with an outstretched arm and with mighty acts of judgment.

Exodus 6:6

ONE day a rabbit darted out in front of our car. My husband quickly braked and avoided hitting the little fellow. The next moment, a car hurtled around a corner ahead of us and charged right down our lane. The driver maneuvered into his lane just in time to pass us safely.

When he caught his breath after the near accident, my husband said, "If that rabbit had not caused me to step on the brakes, we would have been far enough along for that car to hit us head-on. God knew what was going to happen. I believe he sent the rabbit."

Before we had left on our trip, we had prayed and asked God to keep us safe. He knew the exact moment when we needed an answer to that prayer, and he sent the rabbit just in time.

The Facts, Please!

1. *Bricks.* In ancient times in Egypt, people used bricks for building their towns and cities. They were made from clay, water, and chopped straw. A good clay source was necessary. Acids from the decomposing straw acted like a binder to keep the clay from cracking or warping.
2. *Straw.* People gathered straw from fields or threshing floors. It was usually the dried stalks of different grains, like wheat, barley, or millet. Sometimes it came from wild grasses.
3. *Brick making.* Workers chopped the straw into small pieces. They added it to mud and water and trampled the mixture with their feet to blend it well. They pressed this into wooden molds to shape the bricks. When they removed the molds, they laid the bricks in the sun to dry.
4. *Brick makers.* If available, slaves were used for the strenuous work of brick making. The pharaoh in Egypt forced the Israelites to do this work.

Bible Story: A Tough Job Gets Tougher
Exodus 1:1-14; 5:1–6:12; 7:1–12:42

"There are too many Israelites in our land," the pharaoh of Egypt told his leaders. "We must handle them wisely, or they will become powerful and join our enemies if war breaks out." The Egyptians came up with a plan. They chose slave masters, who forced the Israelites to be their slaves.

Out in the desert God told Moses, "Return to Egypt and lead the Israelites out of the land. I promise to be with you and bring you out." Moses went to Egypt and met with the Israelite leaders. He told them what God had said. They believed Moses and worshiped God in thanksgiving.

Next Moses went to Pharaoh. "Our God says we must go into the desert for three days to offer sacrifices to him," he said.

"No! I will not let you go," Pharaoh replied. "You just want to get out of working." He said to the slave masters, "Do not give the slaves straw for making bricks anymore. They must gather their own straw and make as many bricks as before."

The slaves hunted all over Egypt for straw. When they didn't have time to make as many bricks as before, the slave masters beat the Israelite foremen. The foremen complained to Pharaoh, who said, "You're lazy! Get back to work."

The foremen told Moses their troubles. "We are worse off than before," they said. "You have not rescued your people at all." It seemed that God was not keeping his word, because he didn't bring the Israelites out of Egypt at once. But God did it in his own time. First he sent ten terrible plagues on the Egyptians. Then Pharaoh let them go, and they escaped from him forever.

This Is for You

When the Israelites heard that God would deliver them out of Egypt, they wanted to leave right then. They became upset when they had to wait. God doesn't work on our time. He works on his time. He is never too early or too late. By waiting, he showed the Israelites how great his power was. They remembered that lesson many times later on.

It's easy to get impatient when we pray for something and have to wait for the answer. We figure God isn't going to answer our prayers at all. Sometimes we pray for the wrong things, and God won't answer. But other times God waits to answer at the exact moment when he knows the answer should come.

You can count on it: God keeps his promises. Your part? Pray, believing God to answer. If he doesn't do it right away, keep on praying and believing. Wait patiently for God to answer.

Coded Message:
Is God Slow?

Using the code, place the letters on the lines. The first one is done for you. When you're done, you will have written a verse that tells why we think God is slow sometimes.

1	2	3	4	5	6	7	8	9	10	11	12	13	14	15	16	17	18
M	U	H	G	P	K	W	N	S	T	D	O	E	L	I	R	H	A

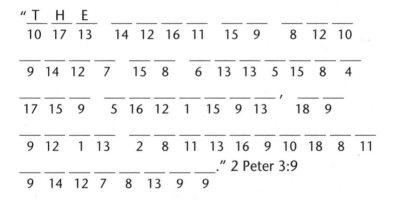

"T H E __ __ __ __ __ __ __ __ __
 10 17 13 14 12 16 11 15 9   8 12 10

__ __ __ __ __ __ __ __ __ __ __ __ __
 9 14 12 7 15 8   6 13 13 5 15 8 4

__ __ __ __ __ __ __ __ __ __ , __ __
17 15 9   5 16 12 1 15 9 13   18 9

__ __ __ __ __ __ __ __ __ __ __ __ __ __
 9 12 1 13   2 8 11 13 16 9 10 18 8 11

__ __ __ __ __ __ __ __ ." 2 Peter 3:9
 9 14 12 7 8 13 9 9

Why do we think God is slow? Because we don't
_____ time the way he does.

6

Food on the Ground and in the Air

Introduction

They asked, and he brought them quail and satisfied them with the bread of heaven.

Psalm 105:40

Come, children; it's time for dinner," Mother called.

Soon four hungry children gathered around the table with their parents. The 15-year-old son, Matthew, looked to see what food was on the table. "Beans again—nothing but beans," he grumbled. "Can't we have something else? I'm sick and tired of beans."

Mother sighed. "You know times are hard, and we don't have much money for food," she said. "Those beans were all I had."

It was five-year-old Jessica's turn to ask the blessing.

"Heavenly Father," she prayed, "thank you for these good beans. I like these good beans. Mother makes them taste just right. In Jesus' name, Amen."

Who enjoyed the food the most—the grumbler or the one who thanked God for it? Which person pleased God?

The Facts, Please!

1. *Miracles.* A miracle is a marvelous event that only God can do. It is an unusual happening that cannot be explained by nature or science. People who do not believe in God often try to explain such events as normal occurrences, but their explanations never hold up.

2. *Manna.* God provided this special food for the Israelites for 40 years while they were in the desert. Manna was a small round substance. It was white, and it tasted like wafers made with honey. "What is it?" the Israelites asked when they saw it. The word *manna* means "What is it?"

3. *Quail.* These are brown, speckled, migrating birds. In March they fly northward across the Holy Land on their way to Europe. In September they fly southward to Africa. They arrive in droves along the shores of the Mediterranean Sea. These plump little birds have strong flying muscles for rapid short flights. When migrating, they stretch their wings and let the wind carry them along.

Bible Story: God Feeds Hungry Millions
Exodus 13:21-22; 16:1-36

God led over two million Israelites out of Egypt, going ahead of them in a cloud by day and in fire by night. When the Israelites ran out of food, they grumbled to Moses and Aaron, "You have brought us out here in the desert to starve. We wish we had died in Egypt, where we sat around pots of meat and ate all we wanted."

The Lord said to Moses, "I will rain down bread from heaven for you. Tell the people to gather enough for that day, but no more. On the sixth day they must gather enough for two days."

Moses and Aaron told the Israelites, "God has heard your grumbling. He will prove to you that he, the Lord, brought you out of Egypt. In the evening you will have meat, and in the morning you will have bread." Suddenly the cloud that went ahead of them shone with a brilliant light of God's glory.

That evening quail came down and covered the camp. The people caught them and cooked them for their supper. Everyone had plenty of meat to eat. In the morning, dew covered the ground. When it dried up, the people saw small white things on the ground that looked like seeds. *"Manhu?"* they asked. "What is this?" No one knew what it was, so they called it *manna*.

"Gather about two quarts for each person, and don't leave any for the next day," Moses said. Some greedy people gathered more than they needed and hoarded it. The next day it was full of worms and smelled bad. On the sixth day some people did not gather enough for the Sabbath Day. When they went to gather food that day, there was none.

"Put some manna in a jar to keep as a remembrance of how I provided for you," God told Moses. He did it, and that manna did not spoil. The Israelites kept it for hundreds of years. And many generations of Israelites remembered that God fed heavenly bread to millions of hungry people for 40 years.

This Is for You

Who brought the Israelites out of their slavery in Egypt? Who opened up the Red Sea so they could walk across on dry land? Who made bitter water sweet so they could drink it? God did. Had he changed when they were hungry? No. They could have asked their loving God for food, and he would have provided it.

Does God know about our needs? Will he take care of us? Philippians 4:19 says, "My God will meet all your needs according to his glorious riches in Christ Jesus." When God says something, it is true. Then why do we complain and act as if God doesn't care?

Sometimes we want something we think is better than what God provides. We're like the Israelites, who complained later on in the desert that they were tired of the manna. They wished they could eat the kind of food they had enjoyed in Egypt.

God knows what is best for us. When we complain about what he gives us, we don't honor him. Then we may cause sinners to doubt if God is good. Let's thank God for whatever he sends and praise him for his goodness.

Word Search:
God's Provision

The list below is made up of words from the Bible story. Find and circle them in the puzzle. You can go down and across. Use the letters not circled to fill in the blanks in the sentences.

BREAD	DEW	GATHER	HEAVEN	POT	SABBATH
CAMP	FED	GLORY	MANNA	PROVE	STARVE
CLOUD	FOOD	GOD	MEAT	PROVIDED	TWO
DESERT	FIRE	GRUMBLED	MILLION	QUAIL	WORMS

```
P  R  O  V  E  G  L  O  R  Y  G
R  M  S  T  A  R  V  E  I  Q  O
O  I  A  W  I  U  C  L  O  U  D
V  L  B  O  W  M  A  N  N  A  P
I  L  B  H  O  B  M  G  M  I  O
D  I  A  E  R  L  P  A  E  L  T
E  O  T  A  M  E  A  T  F  F  F
D  N  H  V  S  D  M  H  I  E  O
D  E  S  E  R  T  E  E  R  D  O
D  E  W  N  M  E  B  R  E  A  D
```

1. God will give ___ ___ what he knows is best for ___ ___.
2. ___ will try not to complain.
3. ___ will thank God for what he gives ___ ___.

Wave the Banners High!

Introduction

May we shout for joy when we hear of your victory, flying banners to honor our God.

Psalm 20:5 (NLT)

Someone is shooting students!" a teacher screamed as she charged into the library at Columbine High School. Cassie Bernall and other schoolmates quickly hunkered down under tables. The two gunmen, also Columbine students, soon blasted their way into the library. There they eventually murdered 12 classmates and a teacher.

Cassie prayed silently, desperately. Then a gunman aimed his gun at her and asked, "Do you believe in God?"

After a brief pause Cassie said clearly, "Yes."

"Why?" asked the gunman. Then he shot and killed her.

Why did the killer ask Cassie this question? Most likely it

was because he knew the answer. She had been a witness for Christ. She carried her Bible to school, she talked about Jesus, and she lived a Christlike life. Cassie flew her banner high to honor her God.

THE FACTS, PLEASE!

1. *Banners.* The banners used in Bible times were of two kinds: (a) flags or streamers made of cloth and figures; (b) devices made of wood or metal. Both kinds were lifted up on poles. Other names for them are *ensigns* and *standards.*
2. *The use of banners.* In Bible times, banners were used as rallying points for military, national, or religious purposes. When a banner was set up on a hill or other high place during a war, it served as a signal for trumpeters to alert troops on a battlefield.
3. *Amalekites.* As the Israelites journeyed through the desert, the Amalekites were living in the southern part of the land God had promised to Israel. They were a wild, fierce band of desert wanderers.

Bible Story: A Living Banner Conquers a Foe
Exodus 17:8-16

After leaving Egypt, the Israelites traveled across many miles of hot, dry desert sand. Then they arrived at a place of rocks, with mountains all around. They did not know it, but Amalekite warriors lurked behind the rocks.

Suddenly arrows whizzed past them. They were under attack! Moses spoke to Joshua, a strong young man, saying, "Quickly choose some of our men and go out to fight the Amalekites. I will stand on top of that hill over there with the staff of God in my hand."

Moses, Aaron, and Hur climbed the hill. Moses lifted up his shepherd's staff with his hands toward heaven and prayed for his fighting soldiers. When his hands were lifted up, the Israelites were able to drive back the Amalekites. Whenever he put his arms down to rest them, the Amalekites gained some ground.

Aaron and Hur saw when Moses was too tired to keep his hands up. They took a stone and put it under him so he could sit down. Then Aaron and Hur, one on each side of Moses, held his hands up. They kept his hands up until the sun set, and Joshua's army overcame the army of the Amalekites.

Then Moses gathered rocks together and built an altar. He called it "The Lord is my Banner."

This Is for You

Moses' hands were like a banner, a living banner, lifted up to the Lord. They showed his dependence on God for victory over the Israelites' enemies. That's why he called his altar "The Lord is my Banner."

We display our country's flag to show we are proud of our country. If we are proud of belonging to God, we will also fly banners to honor him.

Cassie flew her banners to honor God. Her life was a testimony that she loved him. She fearlessly acknowledged her faith in God as she faced death. Cassie's banners have flown so high that all across the nation young people are trusting in Jesus as Savior. Christian kids are wearing T-shirts and wristbands that declare, "Yes, I believe in God."

You may never have to face death for being a Christian. But in your daily living, do you fly your banners high to honor your God? You can never do this on your own. Your enemy, Satan, will easily defeat you unless you pray and depend on God. With his help, you can win the victory and put your enemy, Satan, on the run.

Fill in the Blanks:
Ways to Fly Them High

Fill in the blanks with the letters that follow the ones given (*A* follows *Z*). If you do the activities listed, what will you be flying? Read the letters you have printed down from the arrow to find the word for the remaining blank line.

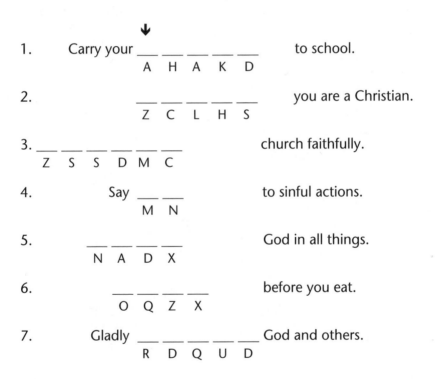

1. Carry your ___ ___ ___ ___ ___ to school.
   A   H   A   K   D

2. ___ ___ ___ ___ ___ you are a Christian.
   Z   C   L   H   S

3. ___ ___ ___ ___ ___ ___ church faithfully.
   Z   S   S   D   M   C

4. Say ___ ___ to sinful actions.
   M   N

5. ___ ___ ___ ___ God in all things.
   N   A   D   X

6. ___ ___ ___ ___ before you eat.
   O   Q   Z   X

7. Gladly ___ ___ ___ ___ ___ God and others.
   R   D   Q   U   D

If you do these things, you will be flying _____ to honor God.

The Strange God in the Tree

Introduction

Our God is in heaven; he does whatever pleases him. But their idols are silver and gold, made by the hands of men.

Psalm 115:3-4

Morio, a young Japanese boy, walked into a temple, the House of a Thousand Buddhas. On either side of a large golden Buddha, smaller Buddhas lined the walls. There were 500 on the right and 500 on the left. Morio walked slowly past the idols, bowing as he went, with his hands clasped together.

Next Morio went outside and faced a big bronze Buddha, 50 feet high. The bronze eyes and ears seemed real to the young boy. He bowed low and then stood in a beam of light that streamed out from a molding above the buddha's nose. "Surely good luck and long life will come to me now," Morio said as he headed for home.

People in India also think there are many gods. A Christian child from India once said to a missionary, "The Hindu young people brag that they have thousands of gods, and we Christians have only one. How can I answer them?" Then she immediately answered her own question: "Of course Jesus is the only true God, and he is living! Their gods are dead."

The Facts, Please!

1. *Idols.* An idol is a false god, something people have made as a substitute for the real God. It is a statue that represents a god or goddess. In Bible times idols were made from metal, wood, stone, clay, or perhaps other materials. They were carved, molded, poured, or shaped by hand.
2. *Idolatry.* This is the practice of worshiping idols. It is the worship of something created instead of the Creator God. The Israelites were the only people in ancient times who did not worship idols, and many times they slipped into the practice also.
3. *The Ten Commandments.* Idol worship is such a serious matter with God that he deals with it in the first two commandments.

Bible Story: He Bowed to a Block of Wood
Isaiah 44:9-20; Psalm 115:1-8

The prophet Isaiah saw people who claimed to be God's children bowing down to idols. They did what the heathen people did. He wrote about this in the book of Isaiah, a part of our Bible. His words show how foolish idol worship is.

He tells about a man who goes out into the forest and looks for just the right tree. It might be a cypress or an oak, or perhaps he cuts down the cedar that he planted long ago. He takes the wood of the tree home with him.

From half of the wood he builds a fire, roasts his meat, and bakes his bread. He also warms himself with the fire. Then he takes the other half of the wood, measuring and marking it. With a tool, he carves the figure of a man.

He has made an idol that can't even move from its place. Yet he thinks he has made a god for people to worship. He falls down in front of it, worshiping and praying to it. "Save me!" he prays. "You are my god."

Not once does the man stop to think that his idol is just a block of wood. It has a mouth, but it can't talk. It has eyes, but it can't see. It can't hear with its ears, smell with its nose, feel with its hands, or walk with its feet. Isaiah says the poor, misled man is trusting in something that cannot help him. Yet he never once asks, "Isn't this thing I hold in my hand a lie?"

This Is for You

Would we bow down to an idol, something that a person made from wood, metal, or stone? We know better than that, don't we? We know who the real God is, and we worship him. But let's stop and think a minute. What is an idol?

An idol is anything we ourselves make into a god. It does not have to be something made from wood or metal. It is anything that comes between us and God. It is anything we love more than we love God.

Our idol might be family, friends, possessions, or pleasures. It might be our plans for our future. If we don't witness for Christ and boldly take a stand against wrong, our fear or pride may be letting popularity come between us and God.

In heathen lands, idol worshipers who learn to trust Jesus as Savior destroy their idols. Have you discovered that you are worshiping an idol? Then put Jesus first (ahead of everyone and everything). In that way, you will destroy your idols.

Crossword Puzzle:
Love the Lord Your God

All the words in the list below are in Luke 10:27. Fit them into the crossword puzzle and then write them on the blanks in the verse.

ALL	HEART	MIND	STRENGTH	YOUR
AS	LORD	NEIGHBOR	THE	YOURSELF
GOD	LOVE	SOUL	WITH	

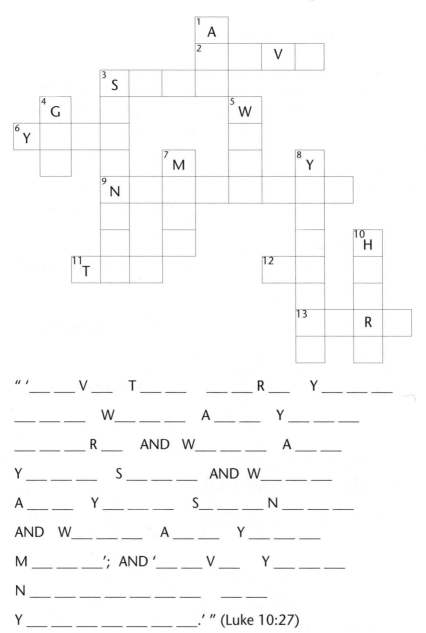

" '__ __ V __ T __ __ __ __ R __ Y __ __ __

__ __ __ W__ __ __ A __ __ Y __ __ __

__ __ __ R __ AND W__ __ __ A __ __

Y __ __ __ S __ __ __ AND W__ __ __

A __ __ Y __ __ __ S__ __ __ N __ __ __

AND W__ __ __ A __ __ Y __ __ __

M __ __ __'; AND '__ __ V __ Y __ __ __

N __ __ __ __ __ __ __ __ __

Y __ __ __ __ __ __ __.' " (Luke 10:27)

9

A Golden Calf and Two Broken Tablets

Introduction

Do not be deceived: God cannot be mocked. A man reaps what he sows.

Galatians 6:7

RACHEL Asibuna lived in Zaire (now Congo), Africa. When she came to live at a mission station, she brought some tiny blue beads with her. She thought they were seeds, so she planted them and frequently watered them. Every few days she carefully took some of the soil away to see if her "seeds" were sprouting. Of course, not one bead ever made a plant.

Rachel didn't reap any plants, because she didn't sow any plant seeds. She just got what she sowed—blue beads. The Bible says that if we live only to please our sinful desires, we will reap what sin brings—destruction and death. We get what we sow, only much worse. If we live to please the Holy Spirit, we will reap the harvest he gives—eternal life.

The Israelites learned a bitter lesson about sowing and reaping.

The Facts, Please!

1. *Calf.* A calf is a young bull (male) or cow (female). Calves were used by the Israelites in the Old Testament for eating and for offering sacrifices to God. In Egypt and in many other places, bulls were worshiped as gods.
4. *Gold.* The precious metal that the Bible mentions most often is gold. God told the Israelites to ask their Egyptian neighbors for silver and gold before they left that land. God caused the people of Egypt to think favorably of the Israelites and to give them all they asked for. *(They deserved far more than that for all their slave labor!)*
5. *Two tablets of stone.* God wrote the Ten Commandments on two stone tablets with his own finger.

Bible Story: The Dance of Death
Exodus 19:16-25; 20:1-21; 24:13-18; 32:1-35

Lightning flashed, thunder boomed, and the sound of a trumpet blasted loudly on the top of Mt. Sinai. Moses led the trembling Israelites to the foot of the mountain. God had come to its top in the form of fire. As smoke billowed up, the people heard God's voice thunder out the words of the Ten Commandments.

"Do not worship any other gods besides me. Do not make idols of any kind, whether in the shape of birds, animals, or fish, and do not worship them," God said. Then he went on to give the Israelites the other eight commandments.

After that, Moses was on the mountaintop with God for 40 days. The Israelites told Aaron, "We don't know what has happened to Moses. We want you to make gods to lead us."

"Bring me your gold earrings," Aaron said. Aaron melted down the gold. Then he molded it into an idol that looked like a calf.

"O Israel, this is the god that brought you out of Egypt!" the people exclaimed to each other.

Aaron built an altar for the calf. The next morning the people sacrificed offerings to the calf god. Then they celebrated by having a wild party with feasting and drinking.

God told Moses, "Go quickly down the mountain! The people have made an idol and are worshiping it." Moses walked down the mountain with two stone tablets in his hands. On them God had written the Ten Commandments.

When Moses saw the calf and the dancing, he angrily threw down the tablets and broke them. But Moses only broke stones. God's people had broken God's commandments.

Moses melted the calf idol, ground it into powder, and sprinkled it on the drinking water. Then he made the people drink it. About 3,000 idol worshipers were killed with swords. And a plague killed many more. The people learned they couldn't sin and get by with it. They had reaped what they had sowed.

This Is for You

God chose the Israelites as his special people. One day his Son would come into the world through their family line. God gave them the job of writing and preserving the Bible for all generations.

Other nations knew the Israelites claimed to worship the one true God. When his people worshiped false gods, God punished them to correct them and to show them they couldn't get by with a terrible sin like that.

If we have trusted Jesus as Savior, we are God's children. Sinners watch our actions and listen to our words. If they see us sin, they think there is nothing to salvation. It is hard then to win them to Jesus.

When we sin, God will send someone to correct us and to teach us right from wrong. He cautions us not to sin, warning us we will reap what we sow. Let's thank God for his correction, confess our sins to him, and ask him to help us please him always.

Word Maze:
When Is Payday Coming?

We will reap what we sow. Payday is coming. When? Never, tomorrow, or someday? Follow correctly through the letters of *PAYDAY WILL COME* twice to find the answer.

It's true!

10

Ringing Bells or a Dead Priest

Introduction

The sound of the bells will be heard when he enters the Holy Place before the Lord, and when he comes out, so that he will not die.

Exodus 28:35

A BELL is a hollow, metal vessel in the shape of a cup, with a metal tongue called a *clapper*. The bell rings with a clear, musical sound when the clapper strikes it. Bells have been rung for different purposes. A few of these are:

- A church bell rings to summon people to a church service.
- Long ago, a town crier rang a bell as he walked down the street before he made an announcement.

- Sometimes an alarm bell sounds, along with a siren, to warn that an ambulance or a fire engine is coming.
- Different types of alarm-clock bells wake people up.
- In America, the Liberty Bell rang to announce the signing of the Declaration of Independence.

Bells were common in the Holy Land, but the Bible mentions them only twice. The verse at the beginning of this lesson is one of those times.

The Facts, Please!

1. *The tabernacle.* This was a special tent where the Israelites worshiped God. They did this in the desert and also in the Promised Land until the temple was built in Jerusalem.
2. *Priests.* The priests were the official ministers or worship leaders in Israel. They represented the people in front of God. Their special work was to offer sacrifices for sins. They all came from the tribe of Levi.
3. *The high priest.* This priest was the chief priest, the ruler of the house of God. The first high priest was Aaron, Moses' brother. When he died, his son Eleazar took the position, and it was passed down in the family from son to son.
4. *Garments of the high priest.* God gave exact instructions for what the high priest should wear when he went into the tabernacle. This garment represented what his job was—the one who stood between the people and God. On a special day once a year, Aaron wore plain linen clothes.

Bible Story: Are the Bells Ringing?
Exodus 28:31-35

(In the following story, the characters are fictional, but they show how real people worshiped God at the tabernacle.)

Early one morning Father and Joel walked from their tent to the tabernacle. Father carried a lamb in his arms. "This lamb is perfect, with no spots," Father told Joel. "We must not bring a sacrifice to God that has something wrong with it."

They arrived at the big linen curtains, seven and one-half feet high, that surrounded the tabernacle and the court. On the east side, they walked into the outer court through the one and only gate in the curtains.

Joel saw the big bronze altar. He knew they could not go beyond that. Father had told him there were two rooms inside the big tent: the Holy Place and the Most Holy Place. Only the priests could go into the Holy Place. No one but the high priest could enter the Most Holy Place, and he could do that only once a year.

A priest met Father and Joel. Father put his hand on the head of the lamb and confessed his sins. Then the priest offered the lamb as a sacrifice on the bronze altar.

Then Father said, "We will stay here in the outer court for a while and listen for the ringing of the bells."

"What bells?" asked Joel.

"They are tiny golden bells that hang on the hem of the high priest's robe between stitched figures of pomegranates," Father said. "As the priest walks about and does his work, the bells jingle."

Joel had heard about those bells. If they did not ring, it meant that Aaron had died. Joel silently listened to the jingling of the bells. At last Aaron came out again. Joel clapped his hands joyfully. "Look, Father, he is safe!" he shouted. "Listening to the bells was exciting!"

This Is for You

Everything about the tabernacle, the furniture, and the work of the priests had to be perfect. They were a picture of Jesus' death and resurrection, and the plan of salvation. That's why the high priest had to perform his duties exactly right. When the people heard the bells jingle, they knew he was doing everything right.

Sinners today can't see a tabernacle with priests. They do see *you*, though. They see how you act and hear what you say. Do you want them to see Jesus in you? Are you eager to help them know salvation is real and good? Then your actions and words will have to show it.

Are you living so that your "bells jingle" as you serve Christ? If you fail to do right and you do not act the way Jesus would, your bells are quiet. This means your testimony for Christ is dead. If this ever happens, ask Jesus to forgive you for failing. Then begin again to "jingle those bells"!

Find the Message:
Be Like Jesus

Jesus refused to do wrong and always did what was right. Two ways we can be like Jesus are given in Psalm 34:14. Shade out all these letters in the squares: C, H, J, W, X, Z. Write the remaining letters in order from left to right to fill the blanks in the verse.

T	X	U	R	C	Z	N	H	F	R	J	O
X	M	E	Z	H	J	V	I	X	C	H	L
A	Z	J	N	D	H	C	D	X	O	Z	G
O	C	H	O	H	X	Z	D	W	H	J	C

"___ ___ ___ ___   ___ ___ ___ ___   ___ ___ ___ ___

___ ___ ___   ___ ___   ___ ___ ___ ___." (Psalm 34:14)

11

A Goat's Strange Cargo

Introduction

We all, like sheep, have gone astray, each of us has turned to his own way; and the Lord has laid on him the iniquity of us all.

Isaiah 53:6

SINNER stumbled down the Way of Death, bent nearly double under the heavy load of sin on his back. In the distance he saw the Way of Life that leads to heaven. Oh, how he wanted to go that way! But a great ditch separated him from it.

"I have heard that I can walk on the Way of Life if I get rid of my load of sin," Sinner said to himself. "But how can I do that? I've tried being kind to others, going to church, and giving money to the poor. None of those things lift my load even one inch."

Suddenly he came to a cross that spanned the great ditch. At the end of it he saw a Man beckoning. "I am the Savior," he said. "Come to me, all you who are weary and burdened, and I will give you rest." Then he said, "I myself bore your sins on the cross."

At once Sinner knew the Man was Jesus! He remembered hearing that Jesus had died on the cross for the sins of the world.

He bowed at the foot of the cross. "Dear Jesus," he prayed, "forgive my awful sins. I receive you as my Savior."

At once the burden of sin rolled from Sinner's back and disappeared. The Savior reached out his hand. Sinner, now named Believer, took his hand and began to walk the Way of Life.

The Facts, Please!

1. *Goats.* In Bible times goats were treasured as a source of meat, milk, fabric, and leather. Butter and cheese were made from the milk. People carried water or wine in goatskin bottles. Most goats in the Holy Land had black hair, curved horns, long ears, and beards.

2. *A special use for goats.* God said the Israelites could use goats, as well as bulls, lambs, and sheep, in their sacrificial offerings. Very poor people could bring pigeons or doves.

3. *Scapegoats.* A live goat became a scapegoat on the Day of Atonement. The name may mean "far removed" or "going far away." Today the word is used for someone who bears the blame for others' sins or mistakes.

Bible Story: The Lonely Goat in the Desert
Leviticus 16:7-22

(In the following story, the characters, Joel and his father, are fictional, but the events are real.)

It was the Day of Atonement, the holiest day of the year. On that day people fasted and confessed their sins to God. Joel and his father joined the large group of men and boys in the outer court of the tabernacle.

Aaron, the high priest, entered the court, wearing plain linen clothes. He killed a young bull as a sin offering for his own sins. He put its blood in a basin and went into the tabernacle.

Father told Joel, "He will go into the Most Holy Place with the blood and an incense burner filled with fire from the Altar of Incense. He will sprinkle some blood once upon the cover of a special, gold box called an Ark and seven times in front of it." Inside the ark were the tablets of stone on which God had written the Ten Commandments.

When Aaron appeared again, he took two male goats and cast lots to see which one would be an offering for the Lord and which one would be the scapegoat. He sacrificed the Lord's goat as a sin offering for the people. Again, he put some blood in a bowl and went into the Most Holy Place.

"Will he sprinkle the goat's blood as he did the bull's blood?" Joel asked.

"Yes," replied Father. "Keep watching; because he will come out soon." When Aaron appeared, Joel's father said, "Good! This means God has accepted Aaron's offerings."

Next Aaron put some of the bull's blood and the goat's blood on the horns of the bronze altar. Finally, he placed both his hands on the head of the live goat. "He is confessing Israel's sins for the past year," Father whispered. "Now God sees that all our sins have been placed on the head of the goat."

A man led the goat away. "He will take it into a lonely place in the desert and leave it there," Father said.

Joel watched the goat leave with its strange, invisible cargo. He couldn't understand how it could be, but Joel knew God had taken away his sins for the past year.

This Is For You

The lonely goat in the desert is a beautiful picture of what Jesus did for us at Calvary. Our iniquities (sins) were laid on Jesus. All alone, he bore our sins in his body on the cross. None of the crowd around the cross could do anything for him. God the Father turned his back because he could not look at our sins. No one has ever been so lonely as Jesus was then.

God forgave the sins of the Israelites, because they followed his directions on the Day of Atonement. Everything they did pointed to the day Jesus would die on the cross.

We do not need a yearly Day of Atonement. Jesus died for our sins once for all. When we accept him as Savior, he forgives our sins and washes them away forever with his blood.

Have you, like Sinner, come to the cross, asked Jesus to forgive your sins, and received him as your Savior? If not, would you like to do that now? *See the last page of this book.*

Number Code:
Guilty or Holy?

Using the number code, fill in the blanks.

1	T	H	J	L	B
2	I	G	O	S	V
3	Y	E	R	U	C
	4	5	6	7	8

1. ___ ___ ___ ___ ___ never sinned, so he is ___ ___ ___ ___.
  1-6 3-5 2-7 3-7 2-7   1-5 2-6 1-7 3-4

2. All people are ___ ___ ___ ___ ___ ___ of sin.
                    2-5 3-7 2-4 1-7 1-4 3-4

3. ___ ___ ___ ___ ___ ___ ___ ___ ___ our sins in his body on
  1-6 3-5 2-7 3-7 2-7 1-8 2-6 3-6 3-5

the ___ ___ ___ ___ ___ as if he were ___ ___ ___ ___ ___ ___ .
    3-8 3-6 2-6 2-7 2-7   2-5 3-7 2-4 1-7 1-4 3-4

4. If we ___ ___ ___ ___ ___ ___ ___ in ___ ___ ___ ___ ___ ,
       1-8 3-5 1-7 2-4 3-5 2-8 3-5   1-6 3-5 2-7 3-7 2-7

he will forgive our sins and wash them away.

5. Then he makes us ___ ___ ___ ___ in his sight. (See the next
page.)   1-5 2-6 1-7 3-4

6. Those who don't ___ ___ ___ ___ ___ ___ ___ in
               1-8 3-5 1-7 2-4 3-5 2-8 3-5

___ ___ ___ ___ ___ will be ___ ___ ___ ___ ___ ___
1-6 3-5 2-7 3-7 2-7   2-5 3-7 2-4 1-7 1-4 3-4

of their sins forever.

12

Difficult Travel on an Ancient Road

Introduction

I will instruct you and teach you in the way you should go; I will counsel you and watch over you.

Psalm 32:8

WHEN Believer trusted Jesus as his Savior, he began to walk on the Way of Life that ends in heaven. "I will read the Bible every day and pray for God to lead me as I walk," he said.

Believer had an enemy named Satan, who often popped up along his way. He tempted Believer to sin. It was hard for Believer to say no, especially on the days he forgot to read the Bible and pray. If Believer gave in to temptation and sinned, God was not pleased and Believer was miserable.

"Please, dear Jesus, forgive me," he prayed. God did forgive him.

Then he read in the Bible, "The battle is not yours, but God's" (2 Chronicles 20:15).

"Why, I don't have to fight my enemy alone," he said. "I will trust God to help me."

Now Believer wins his battles with Satan. At least he does when he remembers to trust the powerful One who fights for him.

The Facts, Please!

1. *Ancient roads.* In Bible times travel was difficult and slow. Usually people walked. Sometimes they rode on donkeys or camels, or they rode in carts. In early days roads were simple paths. They were made by clearing away obstructions, such as trees and boulders, and by filling in larger potholes. A little later road builders laid down earth and stone, but the roads were still very crude and rough.

2. *International roads.* When the Israelites traveled to the Promised Land (Palestine), there were two main roads. The Great Trunk Road was the most important. It went from Egypt to Damascus and passed through Palestine. The King's Highway lay to the east of the Jordan River.

3. *Edomites, Moabites, and Ammonites.* The Edomites were descendants of Esau, a grandson of Abraham. The Moabites and Ammonites were descendants of Lot, Abraham's nephew. These people were distant relatives of the Israelites and lived on land God had given to their ancestors.

4. *King Og.* This man with an unusual little name was

king of Bashan, a land where the Amorites lived. It was a region east of the Jordan River. The Amorites were wicked idol-worshipers. Og was a giant. His iron bed was 13 feet long and 6 feet wide.

Bible Story: Detours and Battles on the King's Highway
Numbers 20:14-21; 21:10-35; Deuteronomy 3:1-20

Tramp! Tramp! Tramp! Millions of feet marched northward over the desert sands. They belonged to the Israelites and their animals. "You may go now," God had told them. "Your fathers who would not go into the Promised Land are dead."

As they came near the land of Edom, Moses sent word to the king, saying, "We are your relatives. Please let us pass through your country. We will not go through any field or vineyard or drink water from any well. We will travel along the King's Highway and not turn to the right or the left."

"No!" the king replied. "If you try to do it, we will march out and attack you with the sword."

God told Moses, "Do not fight your relatives. Go around their land." So Moses led the Israelites off the King's Highway on a detour around Edom. The same thing happened when they came to the lands of the Moabites and the Ammonites.

At last, on the King's Highway again, they arrived at the land of the Amorites. Moses sent word to Sihon, the king, "Let us pass through your land." Sihon came with a huge army to fight the Israelites, but the Israelites were ready for them with 600 fighting men. With God on their side, they won a big victory.

At the border of Bashan, King Og refused them passage and came with his troops. The Israelite soldiers fought the giant king and defeated him. They took possession of the lands of the Amorites and gave them to two and one-half tribes of Israel.

The Israelites pressed on to the Jordan River and looked across to the Promised Land. Now they knew that at last they were coming to their new home!

This Is for You

Being tempted by Satan can be like traveling on a highway. Staying away from him, on the path God wants us to take, is important because life is a journey. At the beginning each person is traveling on the Way of Death. When we trust Jesus to save us, we begin to walk on the Way of Life and are headed for heaven.

In our journey we may make plans and forge ahead to do what we want to do. But God says, "No, don't go that way. I will show you a better way." When we take his detour around our own way, we will find God's ways are best. If we insist on going our own way, though, we will run into trouble.

We have an enemy, Satan, who tries to stop us from doing what God wants. The Bible tells us to resist him. If we are on God's side and trying to do what he wants, he will help us.

When you have sinned, ask God to forgive you. Then

remember that the battle is the Lord's, and you don't need to be afraid. Trust him to help you say no to Satan's temptations. With God's help, you can win the victory. Someday, when you are home in heaven at last, you will be very glad you went God's way.

Find the Right Words:
Whose Fight Is It Anyway?

The Israelites would have to fight many enemies before they could take possession of the land God had given them. God gave Moses some encouraging words for them. Those words can help us in our fight with Satan. To discover what they are, cross out every word that is given more than two times in the list. The remaining words fit in order (from left to right and top to bottom) on the blank lines.

road	Do	not	road	army	be	giant
army	afraid	king	land	of	sword	king
giant	them	land	road	the	giant	Lord
king	your	land	God	sword	himself	will
fight	army	sword	for	giant	king	you

"_____ _____ _____ _____ _____ _____ ;

_____ _____ _____ _____ _____ _____

_____ _____ _____." (Deuteronomy 3:22)

13

Climb Up Blessing Mountain

Introduction

Today I am giving you the choice between a blessing and a curse! You will be blessed if you obey the commands of the Lord your God. . . . You will receive a curse if you reject the commands of the Lord your God.

Deuteronomy 11:26-27 (NLT)

Two best friends, Timothy and Jason, went to a revival meeting. Timothy received Jesus as his Savior. "I'm so happy!" he said to Jason. "You must ask Jesus to save you from your sins, too."

"Not me," Jason said. "I don't need to do that."

After a while, the two boys drifted apart. Timothy tried to please the Lord with his actions. Jason chose to hang out with a rough crowd and do sinful things.

When the two boys grew up, they lost touch. Timothy became the pastor of a church. One day he learned Jason's story: He became an engineer and made good money. He married and had a family. But he began to drink heavily. Finally, he became an alcoholic. He lost his job, his money, and his family.

Each boy made a choice and received the consequence of that choice. Who chose the way of blessing? Today's Bible story is about choosing a blessing or a curse.

The Facts, Please!

1. *Altars.* In Old Testament times an altar was a table, platform, or elevated place used in worshiping God. Usually sacrificial offerings were placed on altars. Way back at the beginning, altars were made of dirt or stones piled up. In the tabernacle, the Altar of Burnt Offering was made of wood and covered with bronze. The Altar of Incense was made of wood and covered with gold.

2. *Mount Ebal and Mount Gerizim.* These two mountains are located in the part of the Holy Land that was later called Samaria. Mount Ebal is 3,077 feet high, and Mount Gerizim is 2,849 feet high. The tops of the two mountains are about two miles apart. A person who shouted from either mountain might be heard in the valley below.

3. *Amen.* This word is an expression of faith or hearty approval. It is used to show that something is a certainty, with no doubt. It means "Yes! So be it!" The Israelites said the word at the end of prayers or

hymns of praise. Christians say it at the end of their prayers to show they have faith in God to answer them. And they use it to show they agree with statements made by a speaker.

Bible Story: Mount Blessing and Mount Cursing
Deuteronomy 11:26-32; 27:1–28:68; 31:1-8; 34:1-9; Joshua 8:30-35

"I am going to die soon," Moses told the Israelites. "Then you will go into the land God promised to give you." He reminded the people of God's laws, which they were to obey in their new home.

"I am giving you the choice of a blessing or a curse," he said. "You will receive a blessing if you obey God's commands and a curse if you disobey them. When the Lord your God brings you into the land, go to Mount Gerizim and Mount Ebal. On Mount Gerizim proclaim blessings, and on Mount Ebal proclaim curses."

Moses appointed Joshua to be Israel's next leader. Then he climbed up Mount Nebo to its highest point, and God showed him the Promised Land. Moses died there, and God buried him.

Soon after entering the Promised Land, Joshua led all the Israelites to Mount Gerizim and Mount Ebal. He wrote God's laws on uncut stones and made an altar of them on Mount Ebal. Then he offered sacrifices on it. Half of the people stood at the foot of Mount Ebal, and half stood at the foot of Mount Gerizim.

Joshua read the words of the Law in a loud voice. He named the curses that God would send if the Israelites disobeyed his laws. After he named each curse, the people on Mount Ebal called out loudly, "Amen!" When the curses were finished, Joshua named the blessings they could have for obeying God's laws. After each blessing, the people on Mount Gerizim called out, "Amen!"

In all the years that followed, God brought trouble on the people when they disobeyed him. But when they obeyed, God gave them many blessings.

This Is for You

We face the same choice today, don't we? We can obey God or disobey him. He does not force us to obey, but he promises us blessings if we do. He warns us not to disobey, because this will bring us troubles.

We may not have troubles right away if we sin. God gives us time to turn from sin and do what he says. But sooner or later, we will reap the harvest of disobedience. "You may be sure that your sin will find you out" (Numbers 32:23).

Let's choose to climb up "Mount Blessing" and live there. That's the place of obedience to God. There we will receive wonderful blessings from God. He loves to give them to his obedient children.

Coded Verse:
Choose Life or Death

In Deuteronomy 30:19, we find more words of Moses about choices. Fill in the blanks in the verse by writing the letter that follows the one given (*A* follows *Z*).

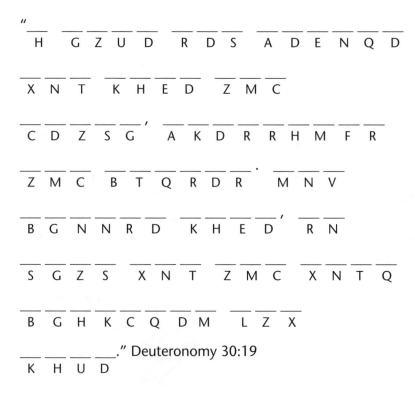

"__ __ __ __ __ __ __ __ __ __ __ __ __
 H G Z U D R D S A D E N Q D

__ __ __ __ __ __ __ __ __ __
 X N T K H E D Z M C

__ __ __ __ __, __ __ __ __ __ __ __ __ __
 C D Z S G A K D R R H M F R

__ __ __ __ __ __ __ __. __ __ __
 Z M C B T Q R D R M N V

__ __ __ __ __ __ __ __ __, __ __
 B G N N R D K H E D R N

__ __ __ __ __ __ __ __ __ __ __ __ __ __
 S G Z S X N T Z M C X N T Q

__ __ __ __ __ __ __ __ __ __ __
 B G H K C Q D M L Z X

__ __ __ __." Deuteronomy 30:19
 K H U D

Strange Battle Equipment

Introduction

Be on guard. Stand true to what you believe. Be courageous. Be strong.

1 Corinthians 16:13 (NLT)

MOM, may I spend Friday night with Melissa?" Becky asked.

"Yes," Mom said. "But remember, Melissa and her parents aren't Christians. Be sure to stand up for what you believe. And don't forget to read your Bible and pray before you go to bed."

Becky promised. But all week long she worried. She wondered if Melissa would laugh at her for reading the Bible.

At bedtime on Friday night, Becky discovered she had not packed her Bible. "Melissa," she said softly, "may I borrow your Bible? I always read the Bible and pray before I go to bed." There! She had said it!

"I don't have a Bible," Melissa said. "I'll get Mom's."

Soon after that, Melissa and her parents came to Becky's church. They told the pastor, "We were embarrassed by Becky's visit, because she reminded us that we haven't been reading the Bible or going to church. Her courage and loyalty to God brought us back to him."

The Facts, Please!

1. *Torches*. For lights, people in Bible times often used torches. A torch consisted of oil-soaked cloths wrapped around one end of a pole and ignited.
2. *Jars (pitchers)*. These containers for holding liquids were usually made of pottery. Most had one or two handles and a spout for pouring.
3. *Trumpets*. The kind of trumpet used by Gideon and his army was probably the ram's horn, called a *shofar*. One use of this horn was to give signals during a battle.
4. *Midianites*. These were nomadic people who roamed the desert. The Midianites were enemies of the Israelites. In the time of Gideon, they oppressed the Israelites for seven years, coming in like a cloud of grasshoppers. They swooped down, stole their crops and animals, and destroyed what they did not take.

Bible Story: A "Weaponless" Army Routs an Enemy
Judges 6:11-16; 7:1-25

A young farmer, Gideon, threshed his wheat one day, hiding out in his winepress. *I hope the Midianites will not see me and take my grain,* he thought. Suddenly a man stood by the alarmed Gideon. He was God, who had come in the form of an angel. "Go and save Israel from the Midianites," he said.

"Me?" Gideon asked. "How can I save Israel?"

"I will be with you, and you will do it," God said.

The Midianites had joined forces with other enemies of Israel. A huge army of 135,000 men had crossed over the Jordan on many camels. They were camped in a valley, ready for war.

When Gideon got an army together, God said, "You have too many men. You will boast you beat the enemy in your own strength."

Gideon told his army, "Those who tremble with fear may turn back." So 22,000 men left, and 10,000 remained.

"There are still too many men," God said. "Take them down to the brook and watch how they drink."

Most of the men got down on their knees to drink. In that position they probably would not have been prepared to fight quickly if an enemy came.

"I will save you with the 300 men who stood on their feet and lapped water from their hands," God said.

That night the little army sneaked up to the camp of the Midianites. They divided into three groups and stood in a

81

circle around the camp. Each man carried a torch inside a jar in one hand and a trumpet in the other. Gideon blew a blast on his trumpet, broke his jar, and shouted. His men did the same.

The startled Midianites awoke. They saw the lights and heard the trumpets. In their confusion, they fought each other with their swords. The ones that weren't killed ran away. God gave the victory to the "weaponless" army of 300 brave men and their courageous captain, Gideon.

This Is for You

Gideon could not believe God wanted him to lead an army against the Midianites. "My family is the weakest in our whole tribe, and I am the least in my family," he said. Still, he obeyed God and faced the enemy.

Becky was a young girl who didn't give up her Bible reading when she visited a friend's house, even though she was afraid her friend might laugh at her.

What did these two people have in common? They had courage and love for God. That's all it took for them to stand true to what they believed. God did the rest, and they were victorious.

Sometimes it takes courage to say we love Jesus. It's much easier to be silent than to be a bold witness.

We can stand firm in the faith because we have the same God as Gideon and Becky had. If we determine to be his courageous witnesses, he will give us the strength we need.

Match-Up:
When Little Is Much

Draw a line from each sentence to its correct ending.

1. The Midianites had an army of   32,000

2. Gideon started out with an army of   300

3. The number of fearful ones was   swords

4. The number of those who drank water on their knees was   trumpets

5. The number who lapped water was   22,000

6. The Midianites had weapons, including   135,000

7. Gideon and his men carried torches and   9,700

How could Gideon's little army do so much? Fill in the blanks with words from this list:

God   trusted   courageously   obeyed

Gideon and his men _____ _____

and _____ _____.

15

Firebrands and Fox Tails

Introduction

I pray that out of his glorious riches he may strengthen you with power through his Spirit in your inner being.

Ephesians 3:16

A TALL, strong basketball player scores more points for his team than any other player has ever done. He makes big money and becomes a hero. His name is known by almost everyone.

A baseball player hits more home runs in a year than any other hitter in the country. He is a national hero.

A big, powerful football player plows his way to the goal line again and again, and his team wins the game. His teammates triumphantly carry their hero off the field on their shoulders.

We admire the strength and might of the best boxers and wrestlers. We give gold medals to Olympic winners. Famous sports figures are praised on television and in the newspapers. After a while, though, their popularity fades, and other heroes take their places. The Bible tells about a hero whose strength surpassed all others—but not forever.

The Facts, Please!

1. *Nazirites.* A Nazirite was a person of either sex who was bound by a vow to be set apart for God's service. This promise could be made either by the person or by the parents of the person. A Nazirite vow could be for a short time or for a person's whole life. While under the vow, Nazirites could not cut their hair, drink alcohol, or go near a dead body.
2. *Philistines.* This tribe of people had settled in cities on the Mediterranean seacoast. They did not worship God, and they were among the Israelites' most dangerous enemies.
3. *Firebrands.* A firebrand was a piece of burning wood, perhaps ignited like a torch by setting fire to a cloth wrapped around one end and soaked in olive oil.
4. *Fox tails.* While there were many foxes in Palestine, the animals called foxes in this story were most likely jackals. These animals resemble the wolf and the fox. They travel in packs. They have an unpleasant smell and make long, mournful howling noises at night. Their bushy tails are about eight inches long.

Bible Story: The Strong Man's Revenge
Judges 13:1-5, 24-25; 14:1-7; 15:1–16:30

Trouble had come to the Israelites. For 40 years the Philistines had ruled over them, plundering their land and making them miserable. Why? The Israelites had been worshiping heathen gods instead of the true God.

One day an angel told the wife of a man named Manoah, "You will have a son. He will be a Nazirite from his birth. You must not cut his hair. Your son will begin the deliverance of Israel from the Philistines."

Manoah and his wife did have a son. They called him Samson. When he grew up, the Spirit of the Lord came on him often and made him very strong.

Samson loved a Philistine woman, which went against Jewish law. On his way to arrange their wedding, a young lion came roaring toward him. Samson grabbed the lion and tore it apart with his bare hands.

After his marriage, Samson left for a while. During his absence, his wife's father gave her to another man.

To get back at them and the rest of the Philistines, Samson found 300 foxes and tied their tails together in pairs. He fastened firebrands between each pair of tails, lit them, and let the foxes go into the Philistines' grain fields. All the standing grain and shocks burned up, along with the vineyards and olive trees. The angry Philistines came after Samson, but he grabbed the jawbone of a donkey and killed a thousand of them.

When Samson loved Delilah, another heathen woman, he told her that his great strength came because he did not cut his hair. While he was asleep, she let a man come in and cut his hair. Samson lost his strength, and the Philistines easily captured him. They gouged out his eyes and made him grind wheat in a prison.

One day, when Samson's hair was long again, the Philistines brought him out of the prison and into the huge temple of their god, Dagon. Samson took hold of two pillars and prayed for strength. He pushed with all his might, and the temple crashed down, killing Samson and about 3,000 Philistines.

This Is for You

God made Samson strong in his body so he could fight Israel's enemies. Samson was weak inside, though. For this reason, he loved heathen women, and he broke his Nazirite vows. If he had been strong and resisted evil, he might have lived longer and done much greater things.

It is good for us to exercise and eat right to develop strong bodies. If we put God first, though, we will be even more interested in being strong inside. On the puzzle page you will find some exercises you can do to give you spiritual strength on the inside. Then your actions and words will show that you truly love God. Even if you don't become a hero in the eyes of the world, one day God will reward you in heaven for your faithfulness.

Fill in the Blanks:
Exercises to Strengthen Your Inner Self

Fill in the blanks in the sentences by choosing words from the list. If you need help, look up the Bible verses on which the exercises are based.

Word List

follow   pray   house   offer   hide   avoid   light

__ __ __ __ God's Word in your heart (Psalm 119:11).

__ __ __ __ continually (1 Thessalonians 5:17).

Go regularly to the __ __ __ __ __ of God (Psalm 122:1).

__ __ __ __ __ every kind of evil (1 Thessalonians 5:22).

Do not __ __ __ __ __ __ the crowd to do wrong (Exodus 23:2).

__ __ __ __ __ your body to God as a living sacrifice (Romans 12:1).

Let your __ __ __ __ __ shine before men (Matthew 5:16).

Write the letters inside the circles here:

_____

Unscramble the letters to answer this question: Who will help us do these exercises regularly and become strong inside?

Answer: The __ __ __ __   __ __ __ __ __ __.

89

16

A Donkey Hunter Becomes a King

Introduction

Now to the King eternal, immortal, invisible, the only God, be honor and glory for ever and ever. Amen.

1 Timothy 1:17

WHAT is the difference between the words *run* and *ruin?*" Mr. Elliott asked his Sunday school class.

"I know," said Susan. "*Ruin* has an *i* in it, and *run* doesn't."

"Right," said Mr. Elliott. "Remember this motto: 'Let Jesus run your life or you'll ruin it.'

"Jesus knows what is best for you always," he added. "Choose to let him be your Ruler."

The next week Susan and her schoolmates took a test. Susan couldn't think of the answer to one question, so she glanced over at another pupil's paper. She decided to copy the answer. Then a little voice in her head said, *Don't do it! You'd be stealing. The Bible says not to steal. "Let Jesus run your life or you'll ruin it."*

Susan tossed her head and thought, *I'm not stealing his answer. He still has it on his paper. Anyway, I won't ruin anything just because I choose to do what I want this one time.* With that, she wrote down the answer. But the teacher saw her copying from the other pupil's paper. For her punishment, Susan had to stay after school and write the answer 500 times. Worst of all, her parents found out and took away her allowance for two weeks.

"I sure made a mess of everything," Susan said to her mom. "Look at all the ruin because I didn't let Jesus run things!"

The Facts, Please!

1. *Donkey.* The little donkey was one of the first animals to be tamed by humans and was the all-purpose beast of burdens in Bible times. Donkeys could carry great weights, usually slung across their backs, in spite of their small size. People could have a safe and comfortable ride on them, so both rich and poor people used them for transportation.

2. *King.* There is only one King who is able to rule perfectly, and that is God. He planned to be the only King of the Israelites, but they never followed him completely. Then they asked for a human king so they could be like other nations. God let them have kings, but he warned them they would have trouble for not letting him be their king.

3. *Anointing.* In Israel, when a person was chosen to be the king, he was anointed with oil. This was done by pouring oil over the person's head. A prophet, acting as God's power and authority, did the anointing.

Bible Story: Tall Saul
Gets a Crown
1 Samuel 9:1–10:27

"Saul, some of our donkeys have run away," Kish said to his son. "Take a servant and see if you can find them." Kish was a rich man who owned many fields and animals. His handsome young son, Saul, was a head taller than any other man in Israel.

Saul and his servant tramped through the hill country and on to other places. They could not find the donkeys anywhere. "We must go back," Saul said after three days. "Father will quit thinking about the donkeys and start worrying about us."

"A prophet of God lives near here," the servant said. "What he says comes true. He will tell us which way to take."

Saul and his servant walked into town. Samuel, the prophet, met them. He knew at once who they were because God had told him about Saul the day before. "When you meet him," God had said, "anoint him to be the king of Israel."

The prophet Samuel took Saul and his servant into a hall for a feast with 30 people. Samuel seated Saul at the head of the table and gave him the best piece of meat. He took Saul and his servant home with him for the night. The next morning Samuel went with Saul toward the edge of town.

"Send your servant away," Samuel told Saul. Then the prophet poured oil over Saul's head, anointing him. "The Lord has chosen you to be Israel's leader," he said, kissing Saul on the cheek.

Later, Samuel called the people together to show them who their king would be, but Saul had disappeared. They found him hiding behind the baggage and hauled him out. The people smiled. What a fine, handsome man he was!

"Long live the king!" shouted the people. At last they had what they wanted—a king!

This Is for You

Saul was a good king at first; but later he disobeyed God and was a bad king. Some of the kings who followed him even led the Israelites to worship idols. The people could have saved themselves many troubles if they had let God rule them.

Let's think about our heart as though it has a throne in it. Only one person sits on a throne as king. If Jesus is our Savior, he wants to be our King. Sometimes, though, we let Self sit on the throne. This happens when we choose to please ourself and do what we want instead of what Jesus wants.

If Jesus rules as King, we have joy and peace inside and God can bless us. King Self can get us into lots of trouble. Jesus tells us in the Bible what he wants us to do. Let's read it and pray every day for God to lead us. We can ask, "What would Jesus do?" Then let's do that and keep him on the throne!

Make a Choice:
Who Is on the Throne?

Below are some statements a young person might make. Print *J* before all the statements that would keep Jesus on the throne of that person's heart and *S* before all that would put Self on the throne.

1. ___ "No, you can't have any of my candy. I want it all."

2. ___ "I know you're tired, Mom. I'll wash the dishes."

3. ___ "I won't go swimming. It's Sunday, and I'm going to church."

4. ___ "Let's play ball instead of going to choir practice."

5. ___ "Wait till you hear this gossip about Mike."

6. ___ "I'll read the Bible first; then I'll play outside."

7. ___ "Let's put these toys in our pockets. The clerk will never see us."

8. ___ "I won't do that, because Jesus would never do it."

9. ___ "I'll see you at the pole for prayer tomorrow."

10. ___ "I'll tell Dad a little white lie to keep from getting punished."

17

A Harp, a Spear, and an Idol in a Bed

Introduction

I love you, O Lord, my strength. The Lord is my rock, my fortress and my deliverer; my God is my rock, in whom I take refuge. He is my shield and the horn of my salvation, my stronghold. I call to the Lord, who is worthy of praise, and I am saved from my enemies.

Psalm 18:1-3

A CLASS of boys was studying about the Bible character Daniel. One boy read Daniel 6:3 aloud. In the King James Version it says, "This Daniel was preferred above the presidents and princes, because an excellent spirit was in him." The boy mistakenly read it, "an excellent *spine* was in him."

Although the boy read the word wrong, he said the right thing about Daniel. That courageous man stayed true to God, even when threatened with death in a lion's den. He had backbone!

This next story is about another Bible character who had an "excellent spine" when facing dangers.

The Facts, Please!

1. *Spear.* In Bible times the two most common battle weapons were the spear and the sword. A spear was a throwing weapon. In close combat, it could also be thrust at an enemy. It had a long, slender shaft with a triangular, pointed metal head.
2. *Harp.* Many musical instruments are mentioned in the Bible. The harp is named the most. Sometimes it is called a *lyre.* It had from three to 12 strings, which were made of stretched sheepskin.
3. *Saul's and David's armies.* King Saul picked strong, brave men to be his bodyguards. These were the start of a group of professional soldiers. David became one of this group soon after he fought Goliath. Later, Saul tried to kill David. He ran for his life, and 600 men joined him to become his private army. When David became king, these men were the beginning of his regular standing army.

Bible Story: An Escape Through a Window
1 Samuel 17:34-50; 18:5-16; 19:1-17

Even as a boy, David was very courageous. While he watched his father's sheep, a lion came and snatched a sheep. David ran after it and grabbed the sheep out of its mouth. When the lion turned on David, he seized it by its mane, struck it, and killed it. Another time, he killed a bear. He fought and killed the huge giant, Goliath, when no Israelite soldier dared to do it.

King Saul made David a captain in his army, and David led his men to fight the Philistines and to win. When people praised David, Saul became jealous; and an evil spirit came on him. David played his harp to help the king calm down. But Saul drew back the spear in his hand and hurled it at David, thinking, *I'll pin him to the wall!* David jumped aside.

David won another victory over the Philistines, and Saul hated him even more. Again an evil spirit came on Saul. When David played his harp, Saul threw his spear at David again. David leaped aside just in time. *Boing!* Saul drove the spear into the wall.

That night David's wife, Michal, warned him, "Saul's men are outside our house. Run for your life or tomorrow they will kill you." She let David down through a window where Saul's men couldn't see him. She put a stone idol in David's bed, covered it, and put goat's hair at the top to look like David's head. Saul's men came, and she said, "David is sick."

When they told Saul, he commanded, "Go back and drag him out. I want to kill him." The men went to David's bedroom and found the idol, but they were too late. David had disappeared.

This Is for You

You've read about just a few of David's brave deeds. For many years God protected him, until King Saul was killed in battle. Then David became the new king.

How could David have been so brave? Read again the verses at the beginning of this devotion. David wrote those verses when the Lord delivered him from the hand of all his enemies, including Saul. David didn't trust in his own strength. He depended on the Lord, who is all-powerful.

We have the same Lord. He can help us when others threaten us because we belong to him. Even if we are afraid, we can count on him to give us an "excellent spine" to be strong and courageous. We can say, as David did in Psalm 56:4, "In God I trust; I will not be afraid."

Find the Missing Letters:
Our Place of Security

In Psalm 18:2, David gave some names for God as his Protector. One of them means "a fortified place, a place of security and survival." Find this name by filling in the blanks with the letter that is missing from each set.

1—P Q R T U V W   2—O P Q R S U V   3—M N O P Q S T

4—J K L M N P Q   5—K L M O P Q R   6—F H I J K L M

7—C D E F G I J   8—L M N P Q R S   9—J K M N O P Q

10—A B C E F G H

__ __ __ __ __ __ __ __ __ __
 1   2   3   4   5   6   7   8   9 10

18

A Cargo of Gold, Silver, Ivory, and Baboons

Introduction

Happy is the person who finds wisdom and gains understanding. For the profit of wisdom is better than silver, and her wages are better than gold.

Proverbs 3:13-14 (NLT)

A FAIRY tale tells of an elf who grants a husband and wife three wishes. They can ask for anything they want. In great excitement and anticipation, the greedy couple tries to decide what their wishes should be. They quarrel and wish troubles on each other, using up their three wishes foolishly. Then they get nothing at all.

Imagine being able to wish for anything we want and getting it! We wouldn't be as foolish as the couple in the fairy tale, would we? Well, maybe we would. It's human nature to be greedy and selfish.

In the Bible, God tells a man to ask him for anything he wants. If God makes an offer like that, we know he will follow through. Wow! What a splendid deal that could be!

The Facts, Please!

1. *Ships.* In Bible times, seagoing vessels were mostly used for cargo. The most venturesome sailors and traders were the Phoenicians, who lived north of Israel. The Israelites were never great seamen, but King Solomon had a large fleet of ships. He hired helpers from Phoenicia. Their skilled craftsmen built his ships and their sailors, who knew the sea, served in King Solomon's fleet with his sailors. Each ship probably had a single mast that held a single square sail. The ships may also have had a bank of oars on each side.

2. *Gold and silver.* Solomon brought huge amounts of gold and silver to Israel on his ships. Gold is the first metal mentioned in the Bible. It is named over 500 times in all. In ancient times silver was valued next to gold. During Solomon's reign he brought in so much of it that it was as common as stones.

3. *Ivory.* Elephant tusks were the source of most ivory in Palestine. It was a luxury item, used mostly by kings and other very wealthy people.

4. *Baboons.* Solomon's zoo probably contained a variety of apes, baboons, and monkeys. He had them shipped in from tropical and semitropical countries.

Bible Story: Why Solomon Became Rich
1 Kings 1:32-40; 3:1-15; 4:29-34; 10:14-29

Before King David died, he told the priest, "Anoint my son Solomon to be king after me." Solomon rode on David's mule to Gihon. There the priest anointed him with oil. The soldiers blew trumpets, and the people shouted, "Long live King Solomon!" As Solomon rode back to Jerusalem, a great crowd followed him, playing flutes and shouting so much that the ground shook.

One day Solomon offered 1,000 burnt offerings on an altar. That night, God appeared to him in a dream and said, "Ask for whatever you want me to give you."

Solomon answered, "O Lord my God, you have made me king, but I'm like a child. I do not know how to carry out my duties. Give me an understanding mind so I'll know how to govern your great people."

God was pleased. "Since you have asked for understanding rather than a long life or wealth, I will give you the wisdom you want. There will never be another person as wise as you. I will also give you riches and honor. And if you obey me, I will give you a long life."

Solomon's dream came true. God gave him such great wisdom and understanding that, like the sand of the sea, it could not be measured. He was wiser than all the wise men on earth. He wrote 3,000 proverbs and 1,005 songs. He taught people about plant life, animals and birds, reptiles and fish.

Solomon also became very rich. He made himself a huge throne of gold and ivory with 12 carved lions on its six steps. He built the magnificent temple for the worship of God, and he built a palace for himself.

Solomon had 1,400 chariots and 12,000 horses. Every three years his ships brought him gold, silver, ivory, apes, and baboons. No one else could match this wise and rich king who asked God for the right thing.

This Is for You

God gave Solomon far more than he asked for because he chose the best thing in the first place. God is not stingy. He loves to give good things to his children. Jesus said in Matthew 7:7, "Ask and it will be given to you." That sounds like what God told Solomon, doesn't it?

We can't take one verse alone and ignore other verses, though. Jesus also said in John 15:7, "If you remain in me and my words remain in you, ask whatever you wish, and it will be given you." If we meet these requirements, we will want the same things God wants. Then we will ask for the right things, and God will give them to us.

It's not a fairy tale. God will give us what we ask for if we belong to him and ask for things that please him. We may have to wait awhile, but God will give us what we ask for—and much more besides.

Coded Message:
What Can God Do?

Using the code, fill in the blanks in this verse that tells what God is able to do.

A	p	m	u	l	a
B	i	r	o	y	t
C	h	n	e	k	h
D	s	w	g	b	c
	1	2	3	4	5

How much is God able to do?

___ ___ ___ ___ ___ ___ ___ ___ ___ ___ ___
B-1 A-2 A-2 C-3 A-5 D-1 A-3 B-2 A-5 D-4 A-4 B-4

___ ___ ___ ___ ___ ___ ___ ___ ___ ___ ___
A-2 B-3 B-2 C-3 B-5 C-1 A-5 C-2 A-5 A-4 A-4

___ ___ ___ ___ ___ ___ ___ ___ ___ ___ ___ ___ ___ ___ ,
D-2 C-3 A-5 D-1 C-4 B-3 B-2 B-1 A-2 A-5 D-3 B-1 C-2 C-3

___ ___ ___ ___ d ___ ___ ___ ___ ___ ___ ___ ___
A-5 D-5 D-5 B-3 B-2 B-1 C-2 D-3 B-5 B-3 C-1 B-1 D-1

___ ___ ___ ___ ___ that is at work within us. (Ephesians 3:20)
A-1 B-3 D-2 C-3 B-2

19

Raven Waiters and God's Groceries

Introduction

I was young and now I am old, yet I have never seen the righteous forsaken or their children begging bread.

Psalm 37:25

Mama, I'm hungry. May I have some toast and jelly?" asked five-year-old Rebecca.

Rebecca's mother sighed. She often could not give her three children everything they wanted. Her husband received only a small salary, and they couldn't buy a lot of food.

"We just ran out of bread, Rebecca," the mother said. "I'll make some biscuits for lunch, but I only have some old bacon grease for shortening." She made the biscuits, and the family ate some; but they didn't taste very good.

That night at dinner, the rest of the biscuits sat on the table. For the blessing, Rebecca prayed, "Dear Lord, help us to eat these biscuits or else send us some better ones. Amen."

Soon the doorbell rang. A member of the church that the family attended was at the door. He ran a bakery route and had a large basket loaded with leftover sweet rolls, buns, biscuits, dark bread, and white bread. "I almost didn't come tonight," he said. "I'm tired, and it's pouring rain. I was tempted to wait until tomorrow night. For some reason, though, I felt I had to come now."

The Facts, Please!

1. *Drought.* A shortage of rain for a long period of time is called a drought. Elijah warned the Israelites not to worship false gods. If they did, God would shut the heavens so it would not rain, and the ground would yield no produce. The result would be a famine and starvation.

2. *Grain.* Bread was the basic food in Israel. The women ground flour from wheat or barley grain, crushing it between two stones. They baked a flat loaf about an inch thick and up to a foot long on hot stones or in an oven. The father broke the bread and served it at a meal.

3. *Oil.* This came from olives, the fruit of the olive tree. It was spread on bread or mixed with flour to make bread. It also had many other uses. Men pressed the oil from the olives in an olive press. One olive tree could grow enough olives to make a family's oil for a year.

4. *Kerith Brook*. This was a small stream near the Jordan River.

5. *Ravens*. Members of the crow family, the gray ravens are native to Israel. They are scavengers.

Bible Story: Food and Drink for a Hungry Prophet
1 Kings 16:29–17:16

One day the great prophet Elijah strode boldly into King Ahab's palace and announced, "As the Lord God whom I serve lives, it will not rain for the next few years until I say so."

King Ahab had built a temple to worship the idol Baal. God was angry about this and had sent Elijah to predict a drought.

"Go east and hide in the Kerith Ravine, east of the Jordan River," God told Elijah. "You will drink water from the brook, and I have ordered the ravens to feed you there."

Elijah hurried to the ravine, away from Ahab, who would surely want to kill him now. Every day, in the morning and evening, ravens brought meat and bread to Elijah. He stayed there, well-fed and safe, until the brook dried up from no rain.

"Go at once to Zarephath and stay there," God said. "I have told a widow there to feed you." Elijah, walking over 50 miles, reached the town on the Mediterranean coast. When he came to the town gate, he saw a woman picking up sticks.

Elijah asked her, "Will you give me a little water to

drink?" As she started to go, he called, "And please bring me a piece of bread."

"I don't have any bread," the widow said. "I have a handful of flour in a jar and a little oil in a jug. I will make a meal for my son and me. We will eat it and die."

"First make a small loaf of bread for me," Elijah said. "Then make bread for yourself and your son. God says your jar of flour will not be used up and your jug of oil will not run dry until he sends rain."

Elijah stayed in an upper room at the widow's house. He and the widow and her son had food every day until the drought ended.

This Is for You

Where did the ravens get Elijah's bread and meat? The Bible doesn't tell us. It's God's secret. What caused the widow's flour and oil not to run out, even though three people ate bread every day? God worked a miracle. Elijah went where God told him to go, and God supplied his needs.

When we need something, we can worry or we can trust God to give us what we need. He may do this through other people. He may even show us how we can meet our own needs. Sometimes we just don't know how God does it, but our needs are met.

If God doesn't give us what we need right away, we can be sure he is doing what is best for us. While we wait, we can learn to be patient and to rely on God more. Our part is to be where God wants us to be and to pray about our needs. Then we can relax and wait happily to see what God will do.

Word Search:
Groceries from God

Below is a list of words from the story of how God supplied groceries for Elijah and the widow. Find and circle these words in the puzzle. You may go up, down, across, backward, or diagonally.

```
F  L  O  R  D  C  R  J  U  G
L  T  A  E  M  D  I  C  L  U
O  T  H  G  U  O  R  D  I  O
U  F  E  E  D  W  I  D  O  W
R  E  L  P  M  B  R  A  I  N
B  E  I  U  A  W  A  E  D  E
R  A  J  H  U  H  V  R  E  A
M  W  A  T  E  R  E  B  H  A
D  W  H  L  O  G  N  I  K  A
O  T  G  O  D  D  S  G  O  B
```

AHAB	DROUGHT	GOD	LORD	RAVENS
BAAL	ELIJAH	JAR	MEAT	WATER
BREAD	FEED	JUG	OIL	WIDOW
DIE	FLOUR	KING	RAIN	

Silent Baal, Frantic Prophets, and Holy Fire

Introduction

Salvation is found in no one else, for there is no other name under heaven given to men by which we must be saved.

Acts 4:12

LET'S pretend we are watching people come to stand in front of Jesus at the Great White Throne Judgment. One man says, "I come in the name of my religion. I was baptized and joined the church."

A woman steps forward, saying, "I come in the name of my family. My parents were good, respectable people; they raised me to be just like them. Our whole town looked up to us."

A young man is next. He says, "I come in the name of my country, which is known as a Christian nation. I tried to obey the laws and honor our flag, and I served a hitch in the army."

On and on they pass by, all of them coming in the name of someone or something they had trusted as their way to heaven. Jesus is sad until he looks toward a large group of Christians who have come to heaven in his name. "I died for the sins of the whole world and rose again," Jesus says. "Those who came to me, repenting of their sins and believing in me as their Savior, are in heaven. No other name but mine is acceptable."

THE FACTS, PLEASE!

1. *Rain.* In Canaan (the Promised Land) the Israelites became farmers. They counted on rainfall and dew to water their crops. Canaan had rainy winters and dry summers. When the autumn rains began in October, the farmers plowed their fields and planted their seeds. If the winter and spring rains came, they had abundant food. If the rains failed to come, they had very little to eat.

2. *Baal.* The Canaanites worshiped Baal, whom they called the god of the storm, springs, and water. They thought it was he who hurled lightning bolts and thundered with his voice. They believed that he tore open the clouds to make life-giving rains pour down. If a drought came, people thought Baal had died and they had to bring him back to life by magic rites. Many Israelites, because they depended on rain, were tempted to worship Baal.

3. *Asherah.* She was the goddess who was supposed to be the wife of Baal. Many women worshiped her.

Bible Story: When Fire Fell from Heaven
1 Kings 18:1-39

After three years of no rain on the parched earth, Elijah stood again in front of King Ahab. "You have brought troubles on Israel," he told the king. "You have disobeyed God and worshiped Baal. Now tell all the people to meet me on Mount Carmel. Bring the 450 prophets of Baal and also the 400 prophets of Asherah."

Soon the prophets and a great crowd of people stood on Mount Carmel. "How long will you go back and forth between Baal and the true God?" Elijah asked. "The one who is God, follow him."

Elijah told Baal's prophets to set up an altar. They killed a bull and put it on the altar as an offering. "Call on the name of your god, and I will call on the name of the Lord," Elijah said. "The one who sends down fire to burn the offering is the true God."

From morning until noon the prophets shouted, "O Baal, hear us!" Nothing happened. They danced around the altar, screaming.

At noon Elijah taunted, "Shout louder! Surely he is a god. He is talking or thinking or traveling. Maybe he is asleep and you must wake him up." The prophets shouted louder and slashed themselves with swords and spears. All day long they cried out to Baal, but he was silent.

In the evening Elijah built an altar of 12 stones and dug a deep trench around it. He cut up a bull and placed it on the altar as an offering. "Pour 12 jars of water over everything," he said. The water ran down the altar and even filled the trench.

Elijah prayed, "O Lord God, let it be known today that you are God in Israel." The fire of God fell. It burned up the offering, the wood, the stones, and the soil. It even licked up all the water from the trench.

When the people saw the fire, they fell to the ground. "The Lord—he is God!" they shouted. "The Lord—he is God!"

This Is for You

Calling on the name of Baal brought no results. He was silent, because he could not answer. He was not God. Calling on the name of anything or anyone but Jesus does not bring salvation. He is the only Savior.

All of us have sinned and don't measure up to the perfect, holy God who created us. Because he loved us so much, Jesus came to earth and was born as a human baby. He was God and man at the same time. He let cruel people nail him to the cross. There he took all our sins on himself. He shed his blood to wash away our sins. Then he came alive again, proving that he is God and can save us.

If by any other name we could be saved, then Jesus wouldn't have had to suffer and die for us. It is by believing on his name alone that we can become children of God. "Everyone who calls on the name of the Lord will be saved" (Romans 10:13). Have you called on his name for your salvation? *See the last page of this book.*

Fill in the Blanks:
The Wonderful Name of Jesus

To fill in the blanks in these verses about Jesus' name, print the letter that follows the one given (*A* follows *Z*).

Therefore God exalted him to the highest place and

___ ___ ___ ___   ___ ___ ___ the ___ ___ ___ ___
 F   Z   U   D   G   H   L   M   Z   L   D

that is ___ ___ ___ ___ ___ every ___ ___ ___ ___ ,
         Z   A   N   U   D   M   Z   L   D

that at the ___ ___ ___ ___ of ___ ___ ___ ___ ___
             M   Z   L   D   I   D   R   T   R

every___ ___ ___ ___ should ___ ___ ___ , in
      J   M   D   D   A   N   V

___ ___ ___ ___ ___ ___ and on ___ ___ ___ ___ ___
 G   D   Z   U   D   M   D   Z   Q   S   G

and under the ___ ___ ___ ___ ___ , and every
               D   Z   Q   S   G

___ ___ ___ ___ ___ ___   ___ ___ ___ ___ ___ ___
 S   N   M   F   T   D   B   N   M   E   D   R   R

that ___ ___ ___ ___ ___   ___ ___ ___ ___ ___ ___ is
      I   D   R   T   R   B   G   Q   H   R   S

___ ___ ___ ___ , to the glory of ___ ___ ___ the
 K   N   Q   C   F   N   C

___ ___ ___ ___ ___ ___ (Philippians 2:9-11).
 E   Z   S   G   D   Q

119

A Tiny Cloud,
a Cloudburst,
and a Fleeing Chariot

Introduction

"Your right hand, O Lord, was majestic in power. Your right hand, O Lord, shattered the enemy."

Exodus 15:6

DAD, I wish we could move into another neighborhood," said Tyler one day as he came home from school. "The gang members that live around here tried to get me in trouble today. They told me to steal some cigarettes for them. They said no one would suspect the preacher's kid of doing anything like that."

"You didn't do it, did you, Son?" his father asked.

"No way, Dad. But some of the boys said they'd pay me back for not doing it."

"I'm sorry, but we can't move," Dad said. "I really believe that God wants us to be here."

That night the family knelt to pray, asking God to protect them. Then they went to bed. Later they heard someone pounding on their door. Loud, angry voices called out, "Tyler, come out here, or we'll burn your house down!"

Dad and Mom came into Tyler's room. "I must go out there," Dad said. Mom and Tyler begged him not to do it, but he unlocked the door and stepped outside. To the angry gang he said, "God sent me here to preach the gospel. God loves you, but he also loves us. If you try to harm us, he will protect us."

Dad walked back in the house and locked the door. The family knelt and prayed again. Then they looked outside. The gang members had vanished!

The Facts, Please!

1. *God's hand.* The Bible speaks of God's hand to help us know what God is like and what he can do. God is *all-powerful.* (He can do anything he wants to do.) God is *all-present.* (He is everywhere all at once.) God is *all-knowing.* (Nothing is a secret from him.) God is *unchangeable.* (He is the same forever.) God is *love.* (He loves with an everlasting love.)

2. *Carmel.* This is a mountain range that juts out into the Mediterranean Sea. It rises from the seacoast to a height of about 470 feet. The Canaanites built temples on Mount Carmel to their weather god, Baal, and other false gods. God sent fire down on Elijah's altar there, proving who the real God is.

3. *Chariots.* These were either two-wheeled or four-wheeled vehicles, drawn by two horses. They were

A Tiny Cloud, a Cloudburst, and a Fleeing Chariot

often used in battles. However, they could not travel well on muddy roads.

Bible Story: A Frenzied Race in a Rainstorm
1 Kings 18:41-46

The fire of God fell on Elijah's altar, and the people shouted, "The Lord—he is God!"

"Go, eat and drink," Elijah told King Ahab. "There is the sound of a heavy rain." So Ahab left to eat and drink. Elijah went up to the top of Mount Carmel again. He knelt on the ground, put his face between his knees, and prayed. Then he told his servant, "Go and look out toward the sea."

The servant went and looked, but he came back to Elijah and said, "I saw nothing."

"Go and look again," Elijah told him. Again the servant said there was nothing. Seven times, Elijah had him look.

After the seventh look the servant said, "I saw a little cloud about the size of a man's hand rising from the sea."

Elijah shouted, "Hurry to Ahab and tell him, 'Hitch up your chariot and go home before the rain stops you!' "

The sky grew black with clouds, a heavy wind rose, and the rain came down in a huge cloudburst. Ahab furiously drove his chariot toward the city. Elijah tucked his cloak into his belt. He ran so fast with God's power that he outran Ahab all the way.

This Is For You

Ahab learned by personal experience what the mighty hand of God could do. He saw the fire that God sent down from heaven. He knew that God held back the rain for three years and then sent a great rainstorm. Still, Ahab never turned from idol worship.

The best way to know what God is like is to see him at work in our lives.

God is all-powerful. We're aware of God's power when we pray for his help and he answers our prayer.

God is all-present. We feel him near us when we trust him and are not afraid in a scary time.

God is all-knowing. God knows everything we need—large or small—so we can rest and be at peace no matter what happens.

God is unchangeable. We understand this when we trust and obey him, never doubting that he will always keep his promises.

God is love. This becomes real to us when we accept his love gift, the Lord Jesus, as our Savior and Lord and experience daily his loving care.

Fill in the Blanks:
What God Is Like

On the blanks across the hand, write the words used in the devotion for what God is like. Unscramble the additional words describing God, with the help of the definitions at left and the Word Bank on page 126.

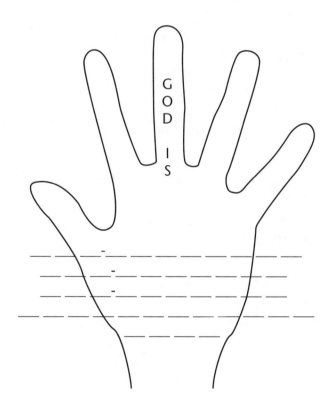

God is also:

Word Bank
Word Bank
Eternal
Holy
Righteous
Spirit
Truth

__ __ __ __ __ __ (invisible, having no body)
T   S   R   I   I   P

__ __ __ __ __ __ __ (living forever; everlasting)
L   E   E   R   T   A   N

__ __ __ __ (separate from sin; sacred)
Y   H   O   L

__ __ __ __ __ __ __ __ __ (being and doing right)
E   R   U   O   S   H   I   G   T

__ __ __ __ __ (the absence of lies)
U   T   T   H   R

The Vineyard of Death

Introduction

Beware! Don't be greedy for what you don't have. Real life is not measured by how much we own.

Luke 12:15 (NLT)

LOOKING around to be sure no one saw her, Alyssa opened her dad's wallet. *Wow! Lots of dollar bills,* she whispered. *One dollar would buy an ice cream cone.*

Alyssa took out a dollar and put it in her pocket. The next morning she saw her mom fixing her school lunch. Without thinking, Alyssa said, "You don't need to put in a dessert. I'm going to get an ice cream cone."

"Where did you get money for a cone?" Mom asked.

"I . . . I found it in the yard yesterday," Alyssa lied.

"Are you sure?" Mom asked. "If you had, I think you would have told me then." Alyssa felt ashamed and told her mom what she had done. Together they decided that Alyssa would have no ice cream for three days.

Because she coveted her dad's money, Alyssa stole, lied, and got into trouble. The Bible tells about a greedy king who ran into trouble for being covetous.

The Facts, Please!

1. *Covetousness.* To covet is to have a strong desire to have something that belongs to someone else. The Tenth Commandment says, "You shall not covet." Many other sins can come from covetousness, like lying, robbery, and even murder.
2. *Inheritance.* God gave the Israelites the land of Canaan as their inheritance from him. After they drove out the idol worshipers who lived there, they divided the land by tribes. Then each family was given a parcel. When a father died, his children inherited his land. According to God's law, an inheritance was to be kept in the family.
3. *Vineyard.* This is an area planted with grapevines. The soil and climate of Israel were well suited for growing grapes.

Bible Story: A Wicked Queen Murders a Vineyard Owner
1 Kings 21:1-19; 22:29-38

Naboth owned a vineyard beside King Ahab's palace. Ahab said to Naboth, "I want your vineyard to use for a vegetable garden. I will give you a better vineyard in its place, or I will pay you what it is worth."

"I can't give up my land," Naboth said. "I inherited it from my ancestors. God said we must not sell our inheritance."

King Ahab strode away angrily. He went to his bedroom and lay on his bed, pouting. He sulked and refused to eat. Jezebel, Ahab's wicked heathen wife, came in to see him. "Why won't you eat?" she asked.

Ahab told her about Naboth and his vineyard. "Is this how a king should act?" Jezebel asked. "Cheer up! Get out of bed and eat. I will get Naboth's vineyard for you."

Jezebel wrote letters to the elders of the city. She signed Ahab's name to them and sealed them with his seal. The letters said, "Call the people to come for a fast. Set Naboth in a place of honor and have two scoundrels lie about him."

At the fast the two wicked men said, "Naboth cursed both God and the king." The angry people dragged the innocent Naboth out and stoned him to death.

"Now you can claim your vineyard," Jezebel told Ahab.

When Ahab came to the vineyard, Elijah met him. "God says, 'Isn't killing Naboth bad enough? Must you rob him too? Where dogs licked Naboth's blood, they will lick yours.' "

Soon Ahab was killed in battle. His blood was washed from his chariot, and the dogs licked it right where they had licked Naboth's blood. It happened as God had said.

This Is for You

King Ahab was very rich. But he was not content with what he had. The Bible says, "Keep your lives free from the love of money and be content with what you have."

Michael had a good pair of athletic shoes, but some other kids had shoes with a popular name label. "I want name-brand shoes too," Michael complained to his folks.

Jennifer liked the new dress her parents bought her until her friend wore a more expensive dress and bragged about it. Then Jennifer was not at all content with her own dress.

God promises to supply our needs, but sometimes things we want we don't need. We may even want what isn't good for us. Trying to keep up with everybody else doesn't bring lasting joy. Being content with what we have does give us joy and peace. What's more, it pleases God.

Crossword Puzzle:
How to Have Great Gain

First Timothy 6:6 says, "Godliness with contentment is great gain." Fit the words *godliness* and *contentment* into the puzzle. Then fill in the blanks with words from the Bible story and place them in the crossword puzzle as directed.

The king's name was _____ (8 down). The king

wanted another man's _____ (2 down). The

vineyardist was _____ (9 across). The king's wife

was named _____ (3 down). The king's wife had

the vineyardist _____ (5 down) to death. The prophet

who came to the king was _____ (6 across). He said

the dogs would lick the king's _____ (10 across). The

tenth commandment is, "You shall not _____" (7 across).

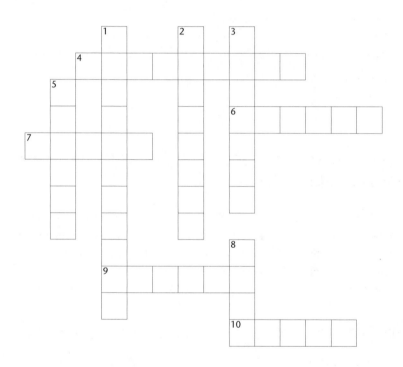

23

Seven Ducks in Dirty Water

Introduction

Cleanse me with hyssop, and I will be clean; wash me, and I will be whiter than snow.

Psalm 51:7

A LEPER has been living outside the camp of the Israelites, but finally his leprosy is gone. He sends for the priest, who examines him. "You are clean," the priest says.

Before the man can go home, the priest must perform a ceremony. He calls for two live, clean birds. He also calls for cedar wood, scarlet yarn, and hyssop (a small, mint-like shrub).

The priest kills one bird over fresh water in a clay pot. He dips the live bird, the cedar wood, the yarn, and the hyssop in the blood. He sprinkles the blood-soaked hyssop over the man seven times. In an open field, he lets the live bird go.

"You are clean from your leprosy," the priest tells the man. "Wash your clothes, shave off all your hair and bathe with water. After seven days, bathe again. Then bring an offering to God, and you may go home." The man does all that the priest says and goes home to live with his family again.

The Facts, Please!

1. *Leprosy.* This word is used in the Bible for several kinds of skin diseases. If a person had the type of leprosy that could infect others, he could not live at home. He had to call out, "Unclean!" when anyone came near. Naaman, in our Bible story, continued to work around other people as the commander of a king's army.
2. *Aram.* This country north of Israel was also known as Syria. Sometimes the Syrians were friendly with the Israelites. Other times they fought against Israel. For many years, Ben-hadad was the king of Syria.
3. *Jordan River.* This is the longest, most important river in Palestine. The distance from its headwaters to its mouth, which empties into the Dead Sea, is 70 miles. But the Jordan River is so crooked that it meanders for 200 miles down its course. It is a very muddy river.
4. *Elisha.* Elisha followed Elijah as Israel's special prophet. God gave him a double portion of Elijah's power.
5. *Ducks.* The Bible does not mention ducks, either wild or domesticated. Look in the Bible story to find what the seven ducks in dirty water are.

Bible Story: A Leprous Skin Comes Clean
2 Kings 5:1-15

Naaman, the general of the Syrian army, had a big problem. He had leprosy. A young slave girl from Israel, a servant to Naaman's wife, said to her mistress, "If only my master would see the prophet in my country, he would cure his leprosy."

Naaman told the king of his country what the girl said. "You must go," said the king. "I will give you a letter to the king of Israel."

Naaman and his servants arrived in Israel at the palace of King Joram. Naaman handed him the letter. It said, "I am sending you my servant Naaman for you to cure his leprosy."

The frightened king tore his robes and said, "Am I God? Can I kill and bring back to life? Why does he think I can cure leprosy? The king of your country is trying to pick a quarrel with me."

Elisha sent a message to Joram: "Have the man come to me," he said. "He will know there is a prophet in Israel."

Naaman went with his horses and chariots to Elisha's door. A messenger told him, "Elisha says, 'Go and wash seven times in the Jordan River, and you will be clean.' "

Naaman became angry. "I thought he would come himself and call on the name of his God and wave his hand over my skin. Couldn't I wash in a clean Syrian river and be healed? The Jordan River is dirty." He turned and started to leave.

Naaman's servants said, "If the prophet had told you to

do some great thing, wouldn't you have done it? Why not wash in the Jordan?"

Down to the river went Naaman. He walked into the dirty water and ducked under it one time. Then he ducked under again and again—seven ducks in all. After the seventh time, his leprosy was gone, and his skin was like a little child's.

Naaman said, "Now I know there is no God in all the world but Israel's God."

This Is for You

In many ways, leprosy reminds us of sin. It was a horrible disease. Sin is horrible, too. It is doing, saying, or thinking anything that does not please God. He hates sin. All people were born with a sin nature (a desire to sin), and all have sinned.

A leper was isolated from others. Sin isolates us, too. It separates us from God.

In Bible times, leprosy could not be cured unless God did it. Sin has no cure either except for the salvation that God provides. The cleansing rites of the priest represent what Jesus did for our salvation.

The leper just believed and let the priest do the cleansing rites. To be cleansed from sin, we believe in Jesus alone.

Jesus died on the cross and shed his blood (the dead bird—see the Introduction to this lesson). He came alive again (the live bird, dipped in blood, which flew away). Jesus' blood cleanses us from sin (the blood sprinkled from the hyssop). Are your sins washed away? *See the last page of this book.*

Fill in the Blanks and Find the Word:
Good News!

There is a Bible word for the good news of salvation. Fill in the blanks with the missing words from John 3:16. Then read down from the arrow to find what the word is.

↓

"__ __ __ so

__ __ __ __ __ the world that he gave his one

and only __ __ __ , that whoever believes in him

shall not __ __ __ __ __ __ but have

__ __ __ __ __ __ __

__ __ __ __" (John 3:16).

The __ __ __ __ __ __ is the good news of salvation.

Bedroom Battle Plans and God's Unseen Army

Introduction

Are not all angels ministering spirits sent to serve those who will inherit salvation?

Hebrews 1:14

A MISSIONARY in Africa had some enemies who hated her because she taught their people about Jesus. One morning these enemies came to her and said, "We don't understand it. Last night we planned to set your house on fire and burn you up in it. When we came near, we saw the house was already burning with a great fire, so we left. But this morning your house is there. It did not burn after all."

"No, it did not burn," the missionary said. "It was never on fire."

"But we all saw the fire," said one man. "This can be

nothing but the work of your God. Will you tell us more about him?"

To protect the missionary, God caused her enemies to see a fire that *wasn't* there. In the Bible, God opened a man's eyes to see an invisible fire that *was* there.

THE FACTS, PLEASE!

1. A*ngels.* These are supernatural, heavenly beings who have more power and intelligence than we do. They are spirit beings and are usually invisible to people. They appeared to some Bible characters in the form of ordinary men and to others as bright, shining beings. Angels are God's messengers. They also serve and praise him around his throne. And, as in this Bible story, God sometimes uses them as soldiers in his army.

2. *Guardian angels.* This is the name we give to the angels who look after God's people. They protect us and help to deliver us from danger. Jesus said that children always have angels watching over them.

3. *The Angel of the Lord.* This angel who appeared to people in Bible times is not a created being (which an angel is). He is the Lord himself, usually in the form of a man, and sometimes wearing the bright clothing of an angel.

4. *Fire.* In some Bible stories God used fire to show his presence and power. Remember the story of the fire falling on Elijah's altar?

Bible Story: Elisha Traps Blind Soldiers
2 Kings 6:8-23

King Ben-hadad was making battle plans to attack Israel again. He told his officers, "We will go to this certain place and camp." He hoped to surprise King Joram, but the king of Israel didn't come near the camp.

Elisha had sent word to Joram, "Beware of going to that place. Ben-hadad's army is there." This happened several times. Ben-hadad called his officers and demanded to know who the traitor was that had told his secrets to the king of Israel.

"We aren't traitors," an officer said. "Elisha tells the king of Israel the very words you speak in your bedroom." King Ben-hadad ordered them to find and capture Elisha.

One morning Elisha's servant, Gehazi, walked outside and saw Syrian horses and chariots surrounding the city. Terribly frightened, he asked Elisha, "What shall we do?"

Elisha said, "Don't be afraid. There are more with us than there are with them." Then he prayed, "Lord open his eyes." Gehazi saw the hills all around Elisha full of horses and chariots of fire. God had sent his angel soldiers to protect them.

When the enemy soldiers came into the city, Elisha prayed, "Lord, strike them with blindness." Immediately, they could not see. "This is not the way you were to come. It is not the right city," Elisha told them. "Follow me. I'll lead you to the man you want."

Elisha led the blinded soldiers to the city of Samaria, the

home of King Joram. Elisha prayed again, and God opened the soldiers' eyes. There they were, surrounded by their enemies!

"These men are our captives," Elisha told King Joram. "Don't kill them. Feed them and send them home." The Syrian soldiers returned home and did not come to fight Israel again for a long time.

This Is for You

Isn't it thrilling to know that God sends his angels to protect us? They are very powerful but not all-powerful, as God is. God uses angels to help human beings. They can travel at the speed of light to do God's bidding. We can remember this when danger threatens us.

Angels worship and praise God, but we are not to worship *them*. We can thank God for them, but our worship belongs to God alone.

Satan and his demons are fallen angels. They once lived in heaven and worshiped God. They rebelled against God, and he cast them out of heaven. Now they tempt us to sin. Let's ask Jesus to help us not listen to them and get tricked into sinning!

Match-Up:
A Review about Angels

Beginning with the words in the first column, draw lines to connect the words that are under the same letter. Read each letter's words in the order of the numbers.

A-1
Angels
are

C-2
spirit
beings

D-2
God's

B-1
Angels
are

A-2
supernatural

B-3
not all-
powerful

C-1
Angels
are

B-2
powerful
but

E-2
and
praise
God

D-1
Angels
are

F-2
the
soldiers

C-3
and
invisible

E-1
Angels
serve

E-3
around
his throne

F-3
in God's
army

F-1
Angels
are

A-3
heavenly
beings

D-3
messengers

25

Holy Incense in Unholy Hands

Introduction

Pride goes before destruction, a haughty spirit before a fall.

Proverbs 16:18

A FROG overheard the conversation of some geese that were swimming in his pond. They talked about flying from the cold north to spend the winter in the sunny south. "Hey," said the frog, "how about taking me with you?"

"How can you fly?" asked a goose. "God provided us with wings, but you can only croak and swim."

"Oh, but I also have a brain," said the frog. "If you will carry out my plan, you will be surprised how smart I am." The geese agreed, and the frog told them to pull up a strong reed in the swamp. When the geese started flying, two of them held the reed by its ends. The frog hung onto the middle of the reed by his mouth.

Up into the air they went, headed south. As they flew over a village, the people saw the strange sight. "Whoever could have thought of such a bright idea?" one of them asked.

The frog opened his mouth and shouted proudly, "I did!"

You can guess the rest. The frog took a great fall because of his pride. The Bible tells about a successful king who was ruined by his pride.

THE FACTS, PLEASE!

1. *Battle arms.* King Uzziah had a large army, equipped with all kinds of weapons of the day. Two kinds were:

2. *A catapult (*also called a *machine)*—a siege engine for throwing stones. It had a huge crossbow on a pedestal that hurled large stones at an enemy or over a city wall.

3. *A sling*—a pair of braided leather straps, joined at one end by a pad of leather or cloth that was large enough to hold a stone. The archer twirled the sling around until there was enough speed for the stone to hit its target. Then he released one strap and the stone flew out.

4. *Altar of Incense.* This altar stood in front of the veil of the Most Holy Place in the temple. Priests burned incense on it two times a day as a picture of believers' prayers. Incense was an expensive mixture of fragrant spices and gums.

5. *Censer.* This was a long-handled container. When

priests placed hot coals in it and sprinkled incense over the coals, a sweet smell wafted through the temple.

Bible Story: The Downfall of a Proud King
2 Chronicles 26:1-23

Uzziah became the king of Judah when he was 16 years old. He reigned for 52 years, longer than any other Israelite king did. Uzziah was a good king who loved and obeyed God for many years.

With God's help, Uzziah waged war against Israel's enemies. He besieged their cities and broke down their walls. He built fortified towers in Jerusalem and in the desert, where watchmen could look out for enemies and defend the country.

The huge army of Uzziah consisted of 2,600 leaders and 307,500 soldiers. He provided them with shields, spears, helmets, coats of armor, bows and arrows, and slings to shoot stones. He placed catapults on his towers and at other defense positions. They were used for hurling large stones.

Then the powerful king became proud, and this led to his downfall. He decided he would be like a priest. He went into the temple and took a censer of hot coals, planning to burn incense on the Altar of Incense.

Azariah the chief priest and 80 other courageous priests stopped him. "It is not right for you to burn incense," Azariah told him. "Only the priests of Aaron's family, who have been consecrated, are permitted to do this. God will not be pleased."

King Uzziah angrily raged at the priests for stopping him. Suddenly, leprosy broke out on his forehead. The priests gasped when they saw it. They hurried him out of the temple. Uzziah had leprosy for the rest of his life. He had to live in a separate house and could never go into the temple again. His son lived in the palace and governed the people.

This Is for You

King Uzziah found out that pride goes before a fall. It cost him his home, his place as king, his power, the honor and respect of others, and God's blessings.

Pride is born in the human heart and grows there. We don't plant it there—it grows on its own. It keeps sinners from trusting Jesus as Savior, because they think others will sneer and make fun of them if they become Christians.

The Bible names seven things God hates, and the first one is haughty eyes (a proud look). When we look down our nose at others and boast about ourselves, God is not pleased. If we think certain people are not good enough for our company, we are not being like Jesus. He is everyone's Friend.

Sometimes we're so proud of ourselves and the crowd we're with that it's easy to make fun of someone who's different. That person can be hurt deeply and may be scarred for life because of our pride. Let's be humble in our thoughts and actions. That's the Jesus way.

Unscramble Words:
To Be or Not to Be

Unscramble the words in parentheses that name some things God does not want us to be (the first letter of each word has been correctly placed for you). Then write the circled letters on the line and unscramble them to discover something God wants us to be.

God does not want us to be:

P __ __ ◯ __ (DROUP), B◯ __ __ __ __ __ __ ◯ __

(ASTFULOB), H __ __ __ ◯ __ Y (HATYHUG), or

◯M◯ __ __ (NAME).

God does want us to be:

_____ H __ __ __ __ E.

26

Jonah's Weird Journey

Introduction

Nothing in all creation is hidden from God's sight. Everything is uncovered and laid bare before the eyes of him to whom we must give account.

Hebrews 4:13

A MAN saw a little boy standing by himself at the end of a city block. He kept standing there, so the man came up to him and asked, "Is something wrong? Are you waiting for someone?"

"No," the little boy replied. "I'm running away."

"Where do you live?" the man asked.

"At the other end of this block. I wanted to go far away," the boy explained, "but I'm not allowed to cross the street by myself."

Thousands of kids and teenagers run away each year. Most of them go much farther than the little boy did. Many end up in a big city, living on the street and running into a lot of trouble. In the Bible, Jonah tells his story about running from God. He got into plenty of trouble!

The Facts, Please!

1. *Nineveh.* This large city northeast of the land of Israel was the capital of Assyria. Nineveh was one of the first cities ever built. Nimrod, Noah's great-grandson, founded it. In Jonah's time, it was very prosperous. A great wall about eight miles long surrounded Nineveh, with its population of 120,000 people. The Assyrians worshiped false gods. They were enemies of the Israelites and often attacked their land.

2. *Casting lots.* In Bible times people cast lots to help them make decisions. This was similar to drawing straws or throwing dice. The lots may have been flat stones, pieces of wood, or other objects. They were probably cast on the ground or drawn from a container.

3. *Great fish.* God prepared a great fish to swallow Jonah. Most likely, it was not a whale, although whales do live in the Mediterranean Sea. It doesn't matter what kind of fish swallowed Jonah. Whatever kind it was, God made it big enough to swallow a man whole and gave it a digestive system that let him stay alive for three days.

4. *Sackcloth.* People who mourned a death or repented of sin wore this cloth, usually made of camel or goat's hair.

Bible Story: A Fish Turns a Wrong-Way Preacher Around
Jonah 1–3

This is Jonah, speaking to you from the belly of a huge fish. Yuck! It stinks in here! It's dark and slimy, and I want to get out. Let me tell you how I got here.

I was a prophet of God in Israel. One day God told me, "Go to Nineveh and preach against it because of its wickedness."

I didn't want to preach to Israel's enemies. I knew that if they repented of sin, God would forgive them. I wanted God to destroy them.

I went to the seacoast, bought a ticket, and got on board a ship. Away we went in the opposite direction from Nineveh. After a while I fell asleep below deck.

The captain woke me up. "Get up!" he said. "Call on your God to deliver us from this storm, or we will all die." I heard the wind howling and the rain pouring down. The sailors cast lots to see which person had caused that terrible storm.

The lot fell on me! I told them I was running from God. "You must throw me overboard," I said. The sailors didn't want to do it. They rowed hard, but the storm got worse. Then they threw me into the rough sea. At once, the storm stopped and the sea grew calm.

I sank down in the water to the very bottom. The seaweed wrapped around my head. I thought my end had come! Then this huge fish swam to me, opened his big mouth, and gulped me down.

I think I've been inside this fish for three days now. I

prayed for God to get me out of here. I repented of my sin and thanked God for delivering me.

Oops! What's happening? Why, I think the fish is spitting me out! Hey, I've landed on the beach. I'm safe! I'll go to Nineveh now, Lord. I'll go right away.

This Is for You

Jonah preached all over Nineveh, saying, "Forty more days and God will destroy this city." All the people believed God and put on sackcloth. They even put sackcloth on their animals. So God did not destroy the city.

Jonah would have saved himself a lot of trouble if he had obeyed God at once.

Do we ever try to run from God? It is impossible to run from the presence of God. He fills heaven and earth. But when we disobey what God tells us to do, we are trying to run from him.

The weather was fine when Jonah's ship set sail. When we first run from God, it may seem that everything is going our way. But God is just giving us time to turn around and do what's right. If we don't, we will have to pay for it sometime.

Jonah's trip began in a ship going the wrong way. God brought him back in a special vessel prepared just for him, and it wasn't at all pleasant. Let's avoid trouble by going God's way always.

Circles and Squares:
Why It Stormed and How Jonah Returned

Circle the first letter in the top row, then circle every third letter to fill in the blanks in the first sentence. Then go back and put a square around the second letter in the top row and every third letter after it to fill in the top row in the blanks in the second sentence.

H S T A E W D N D R T T U A E N

F Z A I L W S G A H J Y T H F O

P R S W O W C M A Y T L I H L F

E O K L W S O H C R I A D M

1. Jonah told the sailors that God had caused the storm because Jonah __ __ __   __ __ __   __ __ __ __

__ __ __ __   __ __ __   __ __ __ __.

2. When Jonah sank into the sea, God __ __ __ __   __

__ __ __ __   __ __   __ __ __ __ __ __ __

__ __ __.

27

Isaiah's Awesome Vision of God

Introduction

Then I heard the voice of the Lord saying, "Whom shall I send? And who will go for us?" And I said, "Here am I. Send me!"

Isaiah 6:8

Do you remember the story of the little red hen? She asked who would help her with the work she needed to do for baking bread. For each task, all the animals said, "Not I."

She did the work herself. Then she asked, "Who will help me eat the bread?"

"I will," said all the animals. Who ate the bread? Only the little red hen and her chicks got to eat it.

God has a task for each of us. He tells us, "Go into all the world and preach the good news to all creation" (Mark

16:15). While God calls certain people to be preachers or missionaries, he expects every Christian to tell unsaved people about him wherever we happen to be.

Only a few respond, "I will." When God passes out the blessings, though, we all want some of them.

The Facts, Please!

1. *Seraph.* This is a kind of angel, a heavenly spirit being. Seraphs are named in the Bible only in this story. They did two things: They praised and worshiped God around his throne, and one of them talked to Isaiah.
2. *Wings.* Most angels probably do not have wings. Usually, when they appeared to people, they came in the form of a man. Seraphs had six wings each. The cherubim were angels with two wings.
3. *Coal.* When the word *coal* is used in the Bible, it usually refers to charcoal. To make charcoal, a stack of wood was covered with earth and leaves. Then it was set on fire. After several days of smoldering, it became charcoal.

Bible Story: "Here Am I. Send Me!"
Isaiah 6–9

Isaiah was one of the greatest prophets ever known. One day he had a special vision from God. Isaiah saw the Lord on a throne, high and lifted up. The train of his robe filled the temple.

Seraphs were above the Lord, each with six wings. With one pair of wings they covered their faces. With a second pair they covered their feet. They flew with the third pair.

The seraphs called to one another, "Holy, holy, holy is the Lord Almighty; the whole earth is full of his glory." The sound of their voices caused the thresholds and doorposts to shake. Smoke filled the temple.

When Isaiah saw and heard all that, he cried, "Woe is me! I am ruined, for I have unclean lips. I live with people who have unclean lips, and I have seen the Lord Almighty."

A seraph flew to Isaiah with a hot coal he had taken from the altar, using tongs. He touched Isaiah's mouth with it and said, "This has touched your lips, and your sin is taken away."

Isaiah then heard the voice of God saying, "Whom shall I send? And who will go for me?"

At once Isaiah replied, "Here am I. Send me!"

Right away Isaiah preached God's messages to the people. He said that God would punish idol worshipers, but he would forgive those who trusted in him. Best of all, he told about a Savior who would come to die for the sins of the world.

Isaiah wrote God's messages in a book. You can find the book in your Bible. It is the Book of Isaiah.

This Is for You

We probably will never have a vision of God as Isaiah did. So how can we know if God wants us to work for him? Well, we know the Bible tells all Christians to share the good news of salvation.

159

If God calls us to do something special for him, the Holy Spirit will let us know. He may speak to us in our heart when we're praying, reading the Bible, or listening to a sermon. It may happen when we read about a missionary or hear one speak.

Isaiah saw holy God and cried, "I am unclean." God cleansed him from sin and used him in a special way. God wants us to live clean lives when we serve him. As soon as we confess our sins, he forgives us. Then he asks, "Who will go for me?"

We can either reply, "Not I" or "Lord, here am I. Send me." Which will you say?

Coded Message:
Whom Shall I Send?

Using the code, fill in the blanks in the poem.

1	2	3	4	5	6	7	8	9	10	11	12	13	14	15	16	17	18
K	A	G	V	W	S	Y	N	M	T	O	E	R	I	H	F	L	D

"___ ___ ___ ___   ___ ___ ___ ___ ___ ___   ___ ___ ___ ___ ___ ,
 5 15 11 9   6 15 2 17 17 14   6 12 8 18

___ ___ ___   ___ ___ ___   ___ ___ ___ ___   ___ ___
 2 8 18   5 15 11   5 14 17 17   3 11

___ ___ ___   U ___ ?"
16 11 13   6

160

"__ __ __ __ __ __ __ __ __ __ __ __ __ __ ,
  5 15 2 10   6 15 2 17 17 14   6   2   7

__ __ __ __ , __ __ __ __ __ __ ?
 17 11 13 18   10 11   10 15 12 12

__ __ __ __ __ __ __ __ __ __ __ __
 10 15 12   15 2 13 4 12 6 10   14 6

__ __ __ __ __ , __ __ __ __ __ __ __ __ __ __
 3 13 12 2 10   10 15 12   5 11 13 1 12 13 6

__ __ __ __ __ __ __ , __ __ __ __ , __ __ __ __
 8 11 10   9 2 8 7   17 11 13 18   15 12 13 12

__ __ __ , __ __ __ __ __ __ ."
 2 9   14   6 12 8 18   9 12

28

Besieging Invaders with Battering Rams

Introduction

There is a greater power with us than with him. With him is only the arm of flesh, but with us is the Lord our God to help us and to fight our battles.

2 Chronicles 32:7-8

The science teacher looked up from the papers he was grading. "Christopher Collins, come up here," he said. "What kind of nonsense is this on your paper? You say God created the universe. Do you think you know more than the scientists of our day?"

Christopher tried to look brave; but inside he trembled. "I don't know more than the scientists, but God does," he replied. "He wrote in the Bible that he created the earth." The teacher glowered, and the kids in the classroom giggled.

"I will not accept a paper like this," the teacher said. "You must write what the textbook says about evolution, or I will not give you a passing grade."

Christopher took the paper. He knew what the theory of evolution taught, but he also knew the truth of God's Word. He wrote what the textbook said. Then he put down these words, "This is the theory of evolution. But the Bible says, 'In the beginning God created the heavens and the earth.' I believe the Bible."

The angry teacher had to give Christopher a passing grade. The young student had proved he knew the material, even though he made it clear that he didn't agree with it. Christopher smiled. He felt very good indeed!

The Facts, Please!

1. *Siege.* In order to go to battle against a fortified city, an enemy would lay siege to it. The enemy soldiers would encircle its walls and then either attack it or wait for the people inside to run out of food and water.
2. *Battering rams.* The first battering rams were long wooden poles. Soldiers would run with them and go up against a wall to break it down. Later, the battering ram was a powerful machine, with a pole suspended on ropes from a tower, sometimes mounted on wheels.
3. *Sappers.* The Assyrian ruler Sennacherib used sappers in his siege warfare against cities in Israel. The sappers were men who dug under a wall, shoring it up with wooden supports. Then they set fire to the supports, and the wall caved in.

4. *Hezekiah.* He was one of the best kings who ever reigned in Judah, the southern kingdom in Israel. He loved the Lord and led his people to worship God, not idols.

Bible Story: A Death Angel Destroys the Invaders
2 Kings 18–19; 2 Chronicles 32:1-33

Sennacherib of Assyria marched into Judah and laid siege to the fortified cities. He destroyed most of them. (Recently people dug up one of the cities and found a letter that Sennacherib had written. It said, "I besieged and conquered by stamping down earth-ramps and then by bringing in battering rams, by the assault of foot soldiers, by breaches, tunneling, and sapper operations.")

King Hezekiah knew that the Assyrians with all their equipment would come to fight Jerusalem next. He prepared for a siege and told his people, "God will fight our battles."

Sennacherib sent his officers and a huge army to Jerusalem. His officers went near the wall and said loudly to the people there, "Don't listen to Hezekiah. Your god cannot deliver you."

The officers also brought a letter for Hezekiah. It said, "The gods of other lands did not rescue their people from my hand. Your god will not rescue you either."

Hezekiah read the letter. Then he went to the temple and spread it out. He prayed, "O Lord, God of Israel, Sennacherib has insulted the living God. Deliver us from his hand, so that all kingdoms on earth may know that you alone are God."

Isaiah sent word to Hezekiah, "God says he has heard your prayers. Sennacherib will not enter your city or build a siege ramp against it. God will defend this city and save it."

That night the death angel came into the camp of the Assyrian army and killed 185,000 men. Then Sennacherib went home, and he himself was killed.

This Is For You

Hezekiah's real enemy was Satan, who hoped to defeat God's people by using Sennacherib and his army. Satan led them to say insulting things against God and to tell Israel to surrender.

Satan uses people to give God's children trouble today, too. He gets them to laugh at us or insult us for being Christians. Through others, he tempts us to deny Jesus or to keep quiet about believing in our Lord.

Hezekiah prayed and believed God would fight for him. We can't fight Satan by ourselves. He is too powerful for us. But God has promised to help us. He is far greater than Satan.

God does not destroy our enemies every time. Sometimes he helps us by giving us courage to stay true to him, no matter what happens. In Matthew 5:11-12 Jesus said, "Blessed are you when people insult you, persecute you and falsely say all kinds of evil against you because of me. Rejoice and be glad, because great is your reward in heaven."

Complete the Acrostic:
God, Our Helper

Reading down in the puzzle, you will find the words to finish the verse. Use the list of words from the Bible story to complete the acrostic.

"I am the LORD, your God, who takes hold of your right hand and says to you, Do not fear; _____." (Isaiah 41:13).

BATTLES   HEZEKIAH   HUGE   INSULT   ISAIAH   LORD
OFFICERS   PRAYERS   SENNACHERIB SIEGE   TEMPLE   WALL

I __ __ __ __ __

W __ __ __
__ I __ __ __
L __ __ __
__ __ __ __ L __ __

H __ __ __ __ __ __ __
__ E __ __ __ __ __ __ __ __
__ __ __ __ L __
__ __ __ P __ __

__ __ __ Y __ __ __
O __ __ __ __ __ __ __
__ U __ __

29

Stolen Treasures and Pure Food

Introduction

Do not follow the crowd in doing wrong.

Exodus 23:2

Kimberly came home from high school one day and said to her mother, "I stubbed my toe at school today. It really hurt, but I didn't say any curse words."

"Why would you even think of saying them?" her mom asked.

"I hear curse words all around me every day at school," Kimberly replied. "The students say them all the time, and the teachers even say them when they are teaching."

Kimberly could not help being around people who cursed. She was determined, though, that she would not be like them. The Bible tells about many people who followed the crowd in doing wrong, and four young people who refused to do it.

The Facts, Please!

1. *Babylonia.* This long, narrow country lay between the Tigris and Euphrates Rivers in the area that is now Southern Iraq. For 700 years Babylonia's neighbor, Assyria, ruled over it. Finally Babylonia gained its independence and became a great empire. Its capital city was Babylon. The people in the land worshiped idols. They conquered many other countries, including Judah, the southern part of the Promised Land.

2. *Treasures.* A treasure is a collection of valuable objects. In Judah, treasures were stored in special rooms in the temple or in the royal palace. These treasures were mostly gold and silver and objects made of those metals. Nebuchadnezzar, king of Babylonia, carried away Israel's treasures and stored them in the treasuries of his gods.

3. *Clean food.* God gave the Israelites special rules about the food they could eat and the way it was to be prepared. He called some animals clean. The people could eat their meat but not the meat from unclean animals. They were not to eat food that had first been offered to idols, because this would show that they believed in the false gods.

Bible Story: Snatched by an Evil King
2 Kings 24–25; Daniel 1:1-21

Again and again, the Israelites turned from God to worship idols, as the people in neighboring lands did. Prophets warned God's people that they would be taken to a foreign land if they continued. Finally, those awful prophecies came true.

King Nebuchadnezzar of Babylon invaded Judah. He took the king, members of the royal family, and some temple treasures to Babylon. After three months, he came again and took away 10,000 people and the rest of the treasures.

Later, he and his whole army besieged Jerusalem for two years until the people inside the city were starving. Then the Babylonians broke down the walls and took away all the Israelites but the poorest ones.

After the first invasion, Nebuchadnezzar ordered his chief official to choose some young men who could be trained to serve him. They were to be good-looking and smart, knowing many things. Daniel, Shadrach, Meshach, and Abednego were among those chosen.

The king sent food and wine from his table for the young men to eat. Daniel and his three friends asked the official for permission not to eat that food.

"I'm afraid of the king," the official said. "Why should he see you looking worse than the others?"

Daniel said, "Test us for ten days. Give us vegetables and water. See if we won't look better and healthier than those who eat the king's food." After ten days, Daniel and his friends did look better than the others. For three years they ate the food that pleased God.

At the end of three years the king could not find anyone equal to the four young men in wisdom and skills. He gave them high positions in his kingdom.

This Is for You

God gave his people special rules about food. Some foods were unclean—they were *taboo,* meaning "to be avoided." God wanted his people to be different from the heathen nations around them. Daniel knew that the king's food and wine were taboo for him and his friends. Daniel 1:8 says, "Daniel resolved not to defile himself with the royal food and wine."

Are some things taboo for Christians? Yes, indeed! God wants us to keep our bodies and lives clean and pure. Such things as taking drugs, smoking, drinking beer, cursing, and looking at dirty TV shows and magazines are unclean. " 'Come out from them and be separate' says the Lord. 'Touch no unclean thing' " (2 Corinthians 6:17).

Some kids may tell you, "Don't knock it until you've tried it." That's not always so. Do you have to be hit by a car to know you should not walk in front of it?

It's hard not to do what other kids are doing, isn't it? You are tempted to follow the crowd so everyone will like you and accept you. Sometimes you may be called "chicken" for not going along with the crowd. Try telling them, "I'm not *chicken;* I'm *Christian.*" Be proud that you follow Jesus and not a crowd of wrongdoers.

Letter Maze:
Who Are You Following?

Today's verse is "Do not follow the crowd in doing wrong" (Exodus 23:2). Beginning with the first row, go through the maze, drawing a line through the words of this verse in their correct order. You may go up, down, right, and left. Then, near the middle of the puzzle, circle the letters of the word to fill in the blanks in the sentence.

T	O	N	O	D	O	W	R
F	D	N	T	O	C	R	I
O	L	H	T	H	E	C	L
T	L	O	W	W	C	F	L
N	O	L	W	O	R	O	W
G	F	J	E	S	U	S	D
I	D	W	R	O	D	N	I
R	W	G	N	I	O	I	N
T	R	W	R	O	N	G	G

We should follow ___ ___ ___ ___ ___ in doing right.

30

Bow to the Image
or Burn in the Furnace

Introduction

**See, I have refined you, though not as silver; I have
tested you in the furnace of affliction.**

Isaiah 48:10

JOHN Hus was a pastor of a large church long ago. He soon
saw that most churches around him were not teaching Bible
truths. In his sermons and writings, John Hus pointed out
the wrong teachings and taught what the Bible really says.

"Stop at once!" the leaders in the other churches
demanded. John Hus continued to tell the truth. Finally the
head of the church took John's name from the church roll
and would not let him be a pastor. Still, John Hus kept on
speaking the truth.

The church leaders chained John Hus to a stake. They

piled bundles of sticks high around him and set them on fire. As the flames rose higher and higher around the man of God, he sang loudly and cheerfully. People could hear him above the crackling and roaring of the fire. At last he was still.

The wicked crowd threw John Hus's ashes in the river. They thought they were rid of him. His teachings lived on, though, inspiring others to preach Bible truths faithfully.

The Bible tells about some other brave men who faced a blazing fire. Did they stay true to God?

The Facts, Please!

1. *Image.* King Nebuchadnezzar set up an image resembling a man. This huge statue was 90 feet tall and 9 feet wide. The king set it up on a plain outside the city of Babylon. The image was gold, perhaps made of wood inside and plated with gold on the outside.

2. *Provincial officers.* The Bible gives a list of all kinds of government officials who bowed to the image. They came from the many provinces that the Babylonians ruled over. They would have spoken many different languages.

3. *Furnace.* People in Bible times used large furnaces for melting metals or for making bricks. These furnaces were made of bricks or stones. In Babylon the furnaces used for making bricks were large enough for several people to walk into them. That kind is most likely the blazing furnace used by Nebuchadnezzar in this story.

Bible Story: Burned-Up Guards and Unharmed Believers
Daniel 3:1-30

Shadrach, Meshach, and Abednego stood in front of the huge image King Nebuchadnezzar had set up. As officials in the kingdom, they had to be there. A herald shouted, "People of every nation and language, when you hear the music, bow to the image and worship it. Those who don't do this will be thrown into a blazing furnace."

An orchestra played, and all the people bowed low to the image. Well, not quite all—some leaders noticed three men who stood up straight and tall.

The leaders hurried to Nebuchadnezzar. "Shadrach, Meshach, and Abednego did not worship the gold statue," they told him.

The furious king called for the three men. "Bow down or be thrown into the furnace," he said. "What god will rescue you?"

"Our God is able to deliver us from the fire," they said. "But if he doesn't, we still won't worship your image."

"Heat the furnace seven times hotter!" the enraged king ordered. He commanded his strongest guards, "Tie them up and throw them into the blazing furnace!" When the guards obeyed, they themselves were burned up from the hot fire.

Soon the king leaped to his feet. "Didn't we throw in just three men?" he asked. "I see four men walking in there, and one looks like a son of the gods. Come out!" he yelled to the men in the furnace. Out walked Shadrach, Meshach, and Abednego.

Everyone looked at them, amazed. The fire had not burned their bodies or singed their hair. Their clothes didn't have any smell of smoke on them. "Here is my new rule," said the king. "If you say anything against the God of Shadrach, Meshach, and Abednego, you will be punished." King Nebuchadnezzar had learned what the true God can do.

This Is for You

The three brave men in this story faced a big test of obedience—to bow or to burn. They would not bow to a false god. They believed God would deliver them. If he did not, they still would not bow down and worship the statue. They passed their test, and God delivered them.

John Hus passed his test, too, but he did burn. Still, he was delivered, because God took him right to heaven. His death inspired many people to be true to God.

All Christians are tested these days, especially young people. You are asked to believe in evolution instead of just creation. In some schools, pupils are told to meditate until they hear a voice in their minds guiding them. This is dangerous because it is not God's voice. In other schools kids may ridicule a Christian who prays at lunch or brings a Bible to school.

If we stay true to God, we may sometimes go through a furnace of affliction or suffering. Then we can remember that there was a fourth man in the furnace in this story. This may have been the Son of God, the Lord Jesus. We will not walk alone in our furnace either. God will be there to give us encouragement and strength. Let's pass our tests with flying colors!

Fill in the Vowels:
Pass the Test and Get a Gift

Find out what gift God will give you at the judgment seat
of Christ if you pass his test of faithfulness to him. Fill in
the blanks in the verse with the correct vowels (a,e,i,o,u).
If you need help, look up the Bible verse listed below.

"B___ f___ ___thf___l, ___v___n t___ th___ p___ ___nt

___f d___ ___th, ___nd ___ w___ll g___v___ y___ ___

th___ cr___wn ___f l___f___." (Revelation 2:10)

31

A Cupbearer Rebuilds a Broken Wall

Introduction

Let us not become weary in doing good, for at the proper time we will reap a harvest if we do not give up.

Galatians 6:9

Do you remember the story of the little engine that did not give up? Pulling a heavy load, it came to a steep hill. People said, "That little engine will never make it up that hill."

The little engine started up the hill slowly, huffing and puffing as the hill grew steeper. "I . . . think . . . I . . . can!" it said over and over. Finally it reached the top and started down. Picking up speed, it rejoiced, "I thought I could! I thought I could!"

The Bible tells us that Nehemiah faced a huge challenge too. Many obstacles stood in his way. Did he give up?

The Facts, Please!

1. *Cupbearer.* A cupbearer poured a king's wine. He was a trusted court official who tasted the wine before the king drank it. If the cupbearer did not get sick or die, it proved that the drink had not been poisoned.

2. *Wall gates.* A city wall had gates in it through which people could enter the city. The gates were usually double doors made of wood and covered with metal. In larger cities, gatekeepers stood by the gates to swing the doors shut and bar them if an enemy approached. People met in an area near a gate to talk, hold court, or sell goods. That's why some gates had names like "Fish Gate" or "Sheep Gate."

3. *Jewish captivity.* The Jews who lived in Judah had kept worshiping idols until God let Nebuchadnezzar take them far away to Babylon. God told some prophets this captivity would last 70 years. Before the time was up, the Persians conquered the Babylonians. At the end of 70 years, King Cyrus let some of the Jews return home.

4. *Artaxerxes (Art-uh-ZERK-sees).* He was the Persian king who followed Cyrus. He let Ezra take a large number of Jews to Jerusalem, and they rebuilt the temple.

Bible Story: The Builders Who Carried Weapons
Nehemiah 1–6

I am Nehemiah, cupbearer to King Artaxerxes in Persia. One day the king asked me, "Why does your face look so sad?" I told him I had received bad news. My home city, Jerusalem, lay in ruins, with its walls torn down and its gates burned.

"What do you want?" the king asked me.

I was much afraid, but I whispered a prayer to God. Then I said, "If it pleases the king, send me to Jerusalem so I can rebuild it." The king agreed! I asked him to give me the help I needed, and he gave it to me.

I made the long trip to Jerusalem. Late one night I went out and inspected the ruined walls. The next day I said to the Jewish officials, "We should rebuild the walls."

"Let's start rebuilding," they said. We went to work. Some men built gates, and others built sections of the wall.

Sanballat and Tobiah, two officials from nearby lands, tried to stop us. First they made fun of us. "What are those feeble Jews doing?" they asked loudly. "Can they bring the stones to life from that heap of rubble? Why, their wall would collapse if a fox walked on top of it!"

We kept building. Then our enemies plotted to bring an army to fight us. When we heard about that, half of our men worked while half stood by with shields, spears, bows, and arrows. Those who carried supplies held them in one hand as they held a sword in the other. Each worker wore a sword by his side.

Nothing stopped us. We built from dawn until the stars came out. We amazed everyone by finishing the wall in just 52 days! People in nearby nations were afraid. "That work had to be done with the help of their God," they said.

This Is for You

Nehemiah and the Jews were determined to build their wall. They let nothing stop them from doing God's work.

God has work for each believer to do, including children. Here is some of his work you can do: At school, learn lessons well and obey the teachers. At church, attend faithfully and learn about the Bible. At home, obey parents, get along well with the whole family, and do chores willingly. On the playground, be kind and unselfish. Don't follow the crowd to do wrong.

Do you find it tough trying to do work for God? The math problems are too hard or the teacher gives too much homework. Maybe you'd like to go with your friends to the beach one Sunday instead of going to church. Perhaps you get tired of taking out garbage and doing other chores. It may be hardest of all when other kids make fun of you for obeying God.

Doing everyday things truly is working for God. Those jobs help you prepare for being a godly adult. With God's help, you can do them faithfully. Don't ever quit. Keep on keeping on like the little train, no matter how big the mountain is that you must climb.

Fill in the Blanks:
Don't Ever Quit

Fill in the blanks in the poem by writing the letter that follows the letter given (*A* follows *Z*).

Don't Ever Quit

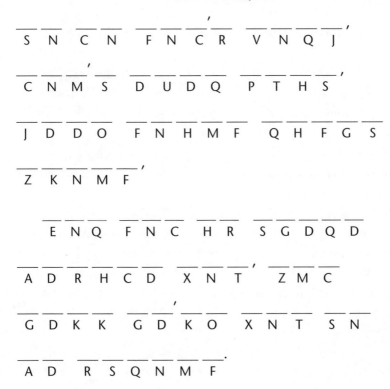

__ __ __ __ __ __ __ __ __ __ __ __ ,
S N   C N   F N C R   V N Q J

__ __ __ __ , __ __ __ __ __ __ __ __ __ ,
C N M S   D   U D Q   P T H S

__ __ __ __ __ __ __ __ __ __ __ __ __ __
J D D O   F N H M F   Q H F G S

__ __ __ __ __ ,
Z K N M F

__ __ __ __ __ __ __ __ __ __ __ __ __
E N Q   F N C   H R   S G D Q D

__ __ __ __ __ __ __ __ __ , __ __ __
A D R H C D   X N T   Z M C

__ __ __ __ __ __ __ __ __ __ __ __ __
G D K K   G D K O   X N T   S N

__ __ __ __ __ __ __ __ __ .
A D   R S Q N M F

32

A Startling Greeting

Introduction

When the time had fully come, God sent his Son, born of a woman.

HEIDI and her grandmother were sorting seeds before their spring planting. Heidi looked at some of the seeds.

"Those are little promises," said Grandma.

"How can a seed be a promise?" asked Heidi.

Grandma pointed to one tiny seed. She said, "This seed promises to be a huge watermelon. We'll plant it, water it, and fertilize it. Then we'll trust God to do the rest."

All through the Old Testament, God promised that one day a Savior would come into the world. He also said this Savior would be the everlasting King. God's promises were like tiny seeds of hope for the Jews. After many years, though, some people let the seeds of hope fall through their fingers. They lost hope.

A faithful few believed that God would keep his promise. They prayed for the Savior to come, and they tried to live for God. One day a startling message came to one of those few.

The Facts, Please!

1. *Four hundred silent years.* After Malachi wrote the last book of the Old Testament, there were 400 long years of silence. God did not inspire any more people to write down his words. No angels appeared with his messages.

2. *Engagements.* In Bible times an engagement was part of the marriage process. Before witnesses, the bridegroom signed papers and gave gifts to the bride and her parents. The engagement lasted for a year. After that a groom took his bride to live in his home. If either person wanted to break the engagement during that year, they had to get a divorce.

3. *Greetings.* When people met one another in ancient times, strangers or those who weren't close friends would say, "Rejoice!" or "Peace be with you!" Good friends might kiss each other on both cheeks or on the mouth. Usually a person of high rank was greeted with a bow, sometimes all the way to the ground.

4. *Messiah.* This is the name the Jews used when they talked about the coming Savior. It means "the Anointed One" and is the same as the word *Christ*.

Bible Story: Good News at Last!
Luke 1:26-38; Matthew 1:18-25

One day a young Jewish girl named Mary sat alone. Perhaps she was thinking about her engagement to Joseph. Suddenly the angel Gabriel appeared to her. Mary was very frightened!

"Greetings, you who are highly favored!" Gabriel said. "The Lord is with you."

Worried, Mary thought, *What kind of greeting is this?*

"Don't be afraid, Mary," the angel said. "You have found favor with God. You are to have a son, and you are to give him the name Jesus. He will be great and will be called the Son of the Most High. He will rule over God's people, and his kingdom will never end."

"How can this be?" Mary asked. "I am a virgin."

"The Holy Spirit will come upon you, and the power of the Most High will cover you," the angel answered. "This Holy One to be born will be called the Son of God."

"I am the Lord's servant," Mary said. "Let it be as you have said." Then the angel left her.

When Joseph learned that Mary was going to have a baby, he was worried. He did not understand that God had given her this child. He thought he should divorce her quietly.

One night an angel appeared to him in a dream. "Do not be afraid to take Mary home as your wife," he said. "The Holy Spirit gave her this child. You will call him Jesus, because he will save his people from their sins." Joseph obeyed God and took Mary home with him as his wife, but he did not sleep with her until her baby was born.

This Is for You

At last, after thousands of years, the long wait for a Savior was over! God sent his own Son to earth, just as he had promised. What great news after 400 years of silence! Mary and Joseph believed God would keep his promise. Now it was happening, and they were a part of it.

Not all God's promises are for everyone. We find out which ones are meant for us by studying the Bible. Also, each promise tells us how to claim it. To get a harvest from a seed, we must plant it and care for it. It's like that with God's promises.

Jesus promised, "You may ask me for anything in my name, and I will do it" (John 14:14).

This means more than ending our prayer, "In Jesus' name." It means to honor Jesus in your life. Want only what he wants you to have. Then you can ask anything, and he will do it. You may have to wait, but God always keeps his promise.

Coded Words:
How to Claim a Promise from God

Using the code, fill in the blanks in the acrostic puzzle. Then, reading down from the arrow, find the letters to fill in the blanks in the last sentence.

1	2	3	4	5	6	7	8	9	10	11	12	13	14	15
A	B	D	E	F	I	M	N	O	P	R	S	T	U	Y

To claim a promise from God,

↓

___ ___ ___ ___ , believing God will do what he promised.
10 11 1 15

___ ___ ___ ___ the Bible to learn about God's promises.
11 4 1 3

___ ___ ___ ___ God in all things.
9 2 4 15

___ ___ ___ ___ God's conditions for claiming his promises.
7 4 4 13

___ ___ Jesus' name is always the way to pray.
6 8

___ ___ ___ , "God's will be done."
12 1 15

___ ___ ___ ___ ___ ___. Don't give up!
4 8 3 14 11 4

Be ___ ___ ___ ___ ___ ___ ___ ___ ___ with what God does
12 1 13 6 12 5 6 4 3

for you.

Remember, God always keeps his ___ ___ ___ ___ ___ ___ ___ ___!

33

Shepherds See a Royal Visitor in a Manger

Introduction

Today in the town of David a Savior has been born to you; he is Christ the Lord.

Luke 2:11

Carmen prayed, "Dear God, I thank you for my new baby brother, Raul, but what I prayed for was a puppy."

People prayed for a long time that God would send the Messiah he had promised. Many of them, though, expected God's Son to come as the king of the Jews. They thought he would lead them to defeat their enemies and bring in peace. They did not ask for a little baby in a manger.

The shepherds, however, were thrilled when they heard the angel's announcement. They believed God had sent his Son at last.

You also can be excited when you read the story again.

Think about how happy God's true children were when they heard the greatest birth announcement ever made!

The Facts, Please!

1. *Shepherds.* Sheepherding was one of the main occupations in all the history of Palestine. The shepherd moved his flock of sheep from field to field to find enough pasture and to locate water for them. The Bethlehem fields were often used to graze the sheep used for temple worship.
2. *Royal visitor.* The baby in the manger was a royal visitor because he was God. The one God is three persons—Father, Son, and Holy Spirit. God the Son always lived in heaven. He had no beginning. On earth he was both God and man. Often we call him by three names—Lord Jesus Christ. *Lord* shows he is God, the ruler of all things and people. *Jesus* means "Savior." *Christ* means "the anointed one." Another name for him is *Immanuel,* meaning "God with us."
3. *Manger.* This was a feeding trough for livestock, located in a stable. We don't know what kind of stable it was where Jesus was born. It may have been under the inn. Perhaps it was in a cave.
4. *Cloths.* Bible-time mothers wrapped their newborn babies in long, narrow strips of cloth, sometimes called "swaddling clothes."

Bible Story: Good News for All People
Luke 2:1-20

Let's hear the familiar story of Jesus' birth as told by the important characters in it.

Joseph: Caesar Augustus made a rule that each person should register for a census in the town where he was born. Because I was born in Bethlehem, Mary and I traveled there. When we arrived, there was no room in the inn, so I took Mary to a stable. I knew she could keep warm and dry there.

Mary: It felt good to lie down on some hay after the long trip. That night my beautiful baby was born. How I loved him! I felt such awe. My baby was God's Son, the promised Savior! I wrapped him in cloths and laid him in a manger.

The angel: I was very honored that God chose me to announce the birth of the Savior. I appeared to some shepherds in the fields outside Bethlehem. The glory of God shone around them, and they were terrified.

I said, "Do not be afraid. I bring you good news of great joy that will be for all the people. Today in the town of David a Savior has been born to you; he is Christ the Lord." Then I told the shepherds that they would find the baby wrapped in cloths and lying in a manger.

A shepherd: I'll never forget that night! All was dark and still when suddenly a brilliant light shone around us. We saw a wondrous angel, who gave us the good news about the Savior's birth—he had come at last! Then the sky was filled with angels, praising God and saying, "Glory to God in the highest, and on earth peace to men on whom his favor rests."

When the angels left, we shepherds hurried to see the baby. We found Mary and Joseph. And there was the baby, lying in a manger! As soon as we left, we told everyone what we had seen and heard. And all of the people were amazed.

This Is for You

The shepherds wanted everyone to know their good news. The promised Savior had come, and they had seen him!

We have even better news to share than the shepherds had. We know that the baby in the manger grew up to be a man, perfect in all his ways. One day he let cruel men nail him to a cross. He took the blame for the sins of the whole world and died in our place. Then he rose from the dead, proving he truly is God.

Now the Savior offers the gift of salvation to everyone. We can accept this gift by believing in him as our Savior and Lord. Then he forgives our sins, and we are saved. Will you share this good news with others?

If you have not yet received the gift of salvation, would you like to do it? *See the last page of this book.*

Word Search:
The Story of Jesus' Birth

Find and circle the words from the list, which are taken from the Bible story. You can go up, down, across, backward, and diagonally.

```
I  L  E  G  N  A  P  E  A  C  E
R  I  L  S  R  Y  H  S  T  G  Y
B  E  B  D  O  T  L  A  C  L  R
J  E  A  R  O  I  O  V  T  O  D
O  S  T  E  M  C  R  I  H  R  A
S  H  S  H  O  A  D  O  G  Y  R
E  T  K  P  L  M  N  R  I  U  K
P  R  Y  E  B  E  A  G  L  B  G
H  A  N  H  I  A  H  R  E  O  O
N  E  W  S  A  N  B  E  Y  R  O
T  T  F  E  L  K  N  Y  M  N  D
```

ANGEL	CITY	GLORY	JOSEPH	LORD	PEACE	SHEPHERDS
BABY	DARK	GOD	LEFT	MANGER	ROOM	SKY
BETHLEHEM	DRY	GOOD	LIE	MARY	SAVIOR	STABLE
BORN	EARTH	INN	LIGHT	NEWS	SEE	

34

Magi, a Traveling Star, and Three Gifts

Introduction

They opened their treasures and presented him with gifts of gold and of incense and of myrrh.

Matthew 2:11

ANTHONY'S dad decided to teach his son about giving to the Lord. One Sunday morning, before Anthony went to his Sunday school class, his dad handed him a quarter and a dollar. "Place in the offering whichever one you choose," he said.

After Sunday school, Dad asked Anthony which he had given. "Well, the teacher taught us a verse that says, 'The Lord loves a cheerful giver.' I knew I could give the quarter a lot more cheerfully than the dollar, so I gave the quarter."

There are three kinds of givers—stingy givers, forced

givers, and cheerful givers. A stingy giver holds a tiny gift over the offering plate and says, "I hate to part with this!" A forced giver sighs and says, "It's my duty, so I'll give this." A cheerful giver bubbles over with joy when the plate is passed and says, "I love giving all I can!"

The Bible tells about some men who gave presents to Jesus. We will see what kind of givers they were.

The Facts, Please!

1. *Magi.* The wise men who came to see Jesus were called *magi.* They were most likely from Persia, east of Palestine. They studied the stars. The Bible doesn't say how many magi followed the star to Jesus. They brought him three gifts, but that doesn't mean there were three magi.

2. *Star.* Some astronomers claim this could have been an exploding star or some other natural event. If so, how could the star have traveled ahead of the magi and stopped over the house where Jesus was? We know that God made this star to guide the magi, and he helped them know it meant the king of the Jews had been born.

3. *Herod the Great.* The Romans were ruling Palestine during Jesus' life there. Herod was the name of several rulers appointed by Rome. Herod the Great ruled when Jesus was born. He was cunning and cruel.

4. *Gifts.* The magi brought three gifts to Jesus: gold, incense, and myrrh. The gold reminds us that Jesus was God's Son and King of the universe. Incense had

a sweet smell and makes us think of the beautiful life of Jesus. Myrrh was used to embalm the dead. It hinted that Jesus would die one day.

Bible Story: Two Warning Dreams Save a Baby's Life
Matthew 2:1-23

One day some magi arrived in Jerusalem and asked, "Where is the one who has been born king of the Jews? We saw his star in the east and have come to worship him."

The news about the magi spread quickly across the city. It reached the ears of King Herod. He was greatly upset. Had a child been born who would take the throne from him or his sons someday? He called for the chief priests and teachers of the law. "Where is the Messiah to be born?" he asked them.

At once they said, "He is to be born in Bethlehem in Judea. That is what our prophets said."

Herod called for a secret meeting with the magi. He told them, "Go to Bethlehem and find the child. Then come and tell me where he is so I may worship him also."

Outside, the magi saw the star. Joyfully they followed it until it stopped over a house. There they found Jesus with his mother, Mary. They knelt down to worship him and gave him gifts of gold, incense, and myrrh.

God warned the magi in a dream not to go back to King Herod. They obeyed and returned home another way.

Joseph also had a dream. An angel appeared and warned him, "Get up and take the child and his mother to Egypt.

Stay there until I tell you. King Herod will look for the child and try to kill him."

Joseph got up at once and told Mary the news. They slipped out of the city that night and escaped to Egypt. Jesus was safe in another land.

This Is for You

The Magi traveled a long distance to see Jesus. They worshiped him and gave him gifts out of their treasures. They were grown men and were probably very rich. But what can a child give to Jesus?

God says in Proverbs 23:26, "Give me your heart." That's the first gift to give Jesus. You give him your heart when you believe in him as Savior. Next, Jesus wants you to give yourself to him. That includes all you own—your body, mind, time, talents, money—everything. When you give yourself to Jesus like that, you make him Lord of your life.

Is it hard to give these gifts to Jesus? It won't be if you remember that he gave his life to save you. He gives you many good things every day, too. You don't want to be a stingy giver or a forced giver, do you? Show your love to Jesus by being a cheerful giver! "God loves a cheerful giver" (2 Corinthians 9:7).

Match-Up:
Gifts to Jesus

Draw these lines: Set 1—from the giver to what was given. Set 2—from gifts you can give to Jesus to ways you can use them for him.

Set 1—What Bible characters gave

Angels

Mary

Shepherds

The Magi

1. worship, praise, and a witness about Jesus

2. messages about Jesus from God to people

3. her body, her love, and her prayers

4. worship and three special gifts

Set 2—How you can use these gifts to Jesus for his glory

Your heart

Your body

Your mind

Your time

Your talents

Your money

1. Study school lessons and the Bible.

2. Develop them and use them for his glory.

3. Invite him to come in and live there.

4. Use every part to please and honor Jesus.

5. Give to the church and elsewhere for God's work.

6. Spend some of it each day reading the Bible, praying, and witnessing.

35

Odd Clothes and Strange Food

Introduction

The next day John saw Jesus coming toward him and said, "Look, the Lamb of God, who takes away the sin of the world!"

John 1:29

I NEED your doll," Vanessa told her little sister, Stephanie. Vanessa grabbed the doll and put it in a bag. They were taking the bag of toys to church to give to kids whose families couldn't afford to buy extra things for them.

"No, no!" yelled Stephanie. "That's my doll. Don't take her!"

"It's a gift," Vanessa said. "We have to give a gift to Jesus."

In another part of the world some English children sent toys to a mission hospital in India at Christmastime. The mission doctor gave their gifts to the poor children in the village.

The doctor told the children about another village. "The children there have never heard about Jesus or Christmas," he said. "Would each of you like to bring one of your old toys for them next Sunday?"

The next week all the poor children brought their new toys for the children who didn't know about Jesus. When asked why they gave the new ones, one girl said, "Jesus gave himself for us. So we can't give him anything less than our best!"

In these stories, who sacrificed to give the best gift? The Bible tells about the greatest gift ever given.

The Facts, Please!

1. *Camel's hair.* Like Elijah, John the Baptist wore clothes made of camel's hair. It was not soft, expensive cloth woven from the fine hairs around a camel's belly. It was rough cloth made of the coarse hair from a camel's back.

2. *Locust.* This is a type of grasshopper with a brown body about two to three inches long. People in Bible times ate locusts boiled, fried, or dried. Desert people still eat locusts today.

3. *Wild honey.* Honey and honeycombs could be collected from holes in the ground or from crevices between rocks.

4. *Lamb of God.* John called Jesus "the Lamb of God." A lamb was one of the animals used for a sacrifice or gift to God. It had to be in perfect shape. People shed

its blood when they offered it, and God forgave their sins. It was a picture of Jesus. He became the Lamb of God when he died on the cross and shed his blood for our sins.

Bible Story: A Desert Preacher Baptizes the Lamb of God
Luke 1:13-17; Mark 1:1-11; 6:17-29; John 1:29-34

"Prepare the way for the Lord!" The voice rang out across the desert sands. Crowds of people from all around flocked to hear this desert preacher. His name was John. He lived in the desert and wore clothes made from camel's hair. He also wore a leather belt. For food he ate locusts and wild honey.

God chose John to be the one who would get people ready for the coming of Jesus. John urged them to turn from their sins. He baptized those who repented. Soon he was known as "John the Baptist."

"I baptize you with water," John said, "but one comes after me who is more powerful than I. He will baptize you with the Holy Spirit."

One day Jesus came to John the Baptist to be baptized. "I am not worthy to baptize you," John said. Jesus insisted, so John baptized him.

As Jesus came up out of the water, heaven opened. The Holy Spirit came down like a dove and rested on Jesus. A voice from heaven said, "You are my Son, whom I love; with you I am well pleased."

Another day John saw Jesus coming toward him. "Look, the Lamb of God, who takes away the sin of the world!" he said.

John the Baptist kept preaching and baptizing. He rebuked the ruler, Herod Antipas, for his wicked living. Herod put John in prison. Later, to please his wife, Herod beheaded John. The great desert preacher sacrificed his life for staying true to God and preaching his Word.

This Is for You

John the Baptist could have chosen a life of doing things only to please himself. Instead, he lived a simple life in the desert and preached God's truth. That was a sacrifice. He gave an even greater sacrifice when he gave his life because of his faithful preaching.

Vanessa wanted to give away her sister's doll. That cost Vanessa nothing. A true sacrifice to God is offering him a gift that costs us something. Jesus, the Lamb of God, died on the cross for the sins of the whole world. That was the greatest sacrifice ever made.

Romans 12:1 tells us, "Offer your bodies as living sacrifices, holy and pleasing to God." In the last devotion we talked about giving everything to Jesus. Sometimes this will mean sacrificing or giving up something that is very special to you.

As the little girl from India said, "Jesus gave himself for us. So we can't give him anything less than our best!"

Double Scramble:
What Jesus Deserves

The sentence is scrambled, and so is each word.
Unscramble the words, and then place them on the blank
lines with the same numbers.

DOGO   STEB   OT   LYNO   IVEG   GOUNEH   YM   SI   SUEJS
  5   3   7   1   8   6   2   4   9

_____ _____ _____ _____ _____ _____
  1   2   3   4   5   6

_____ _____ _____.
  7   8   9

36

Flat Roofs
and Straw Mats

Introduction

Go home to your friends, and tell them what wonderful things the Lord has done for you.

Mark 5:19 (NLT)

Sophie cleaned houses for a living. After she received Jesus as her Savior, she prayed for 12 years that God would send her as a missionary to a foreign land. "But how can I ever get there?" she wondered.

Then God spoke to her heart, "You have a mission field right here. Many people all around you need Jesus."

Sophie began to talk about Jesus everywhere she went. She helped many people learn to follow Jesus. Someone kidded her by saying he had seen her talking to a plastic model in a department store window.

"Maybe I did," Sophie said. "My eyesight is not good. But talking about Jesus to a 'plastic' model is not as bad as being a silent, 'plastic' Christian who never talks to anybody about him."

The Bible tells about four men who not only *told* a friend about Jesus, but *brought* the man right down to him.

ThE FACTS, PlEASE!

1. *Paralytic.* This is a person who is paralyzed—who has lost movement in one or more parts of the body.
2. *Roofs.* In Bible times most houses had flat roofs. Builders laid rough wooden beams across the top of a house and placed a mat of branches over them. Then they sealed the roof with clay, packed down with heavy rollers to make it smooth and hard. A stairway or ladder led up to the roof, where people went for many activities. A low wall around the roof kept the people from falling off.
3. *Mat.* Most Bible people slept on straw mats on the floor. They rolled them up and stored them during the day.
4. *Teachers of the Law.* These men were called *scribes.* They made copies of the Old Testament. They also taught it. Most of them did not believe Jesus was the Son of God.

Bible Story: Through the Roof to Jesus
Mark 2:1-12; Luke 5:17-26

"Jesus has come back to our city!" The word spread quickly through the city of Capernaum. When people learned which house Jesus was in, they hurried there. The crowd, trying to hear Jesus speak, filled the house and the whole area outside the door.

In another house, a paralyzed man lay on his mat. Four of his friends came and picked up his mat by the four corners. Down the street they marched to the house where Jesus was. They hoped Jesus would make their friend well.

The men tried to push their way through the huge crowd to get to Jesus. Perhaps they called, "Make way! Let us through!" But no one moved.

The four men had an idea. Maybe they could drop their friend down through the roof. They climbed up the stairway, carrying the mat. They laid it down and dug through the roof until they had made a hole big enough to let their friend down into the house. He ended up right in front of Jesus.

When Jesus saw the faith of the men, he said to the paralytic, "Son, your sins are forgiven."

Some scribes in the crowd heard Jesus' words. They thought, *Why does this fellow talk like that? No one but God alone can forgive sins!*

Knowing their thoughts, Jesus asked, "Why do you think like that? Which is easier to say, 'Your sins are forgiven,' or 'Get up, take your mat and walk'? I will show you that I have the right to forgive sins." Looking at the man, he said, "Get up. Take your mat and go home."

At once the man stood up. He picked up his mat and walked home, praising God all the way. The amazed crowd praised God, too. "We have seen remarkable things today," they said.

This Is For You

The four men brought their friend to Jesus because they believed Jesus could heal him. No matter how difficult it was, they kept trying until they succeeded. Jesus did heal their friend, and he also forgave the man's sins.

Do some members of your family need to receive Jesus as Savior and Lord? Do you have friends who are not Christians? If you truly love them, you want them to be in heaven with you someday. The very best thing you can do for them is to bring them to Jesus.

There are two things you can do. You can tell them about Jesus, and you can show them how to live for him. Your talk and your actions are both very important. You must back up your talk with a Christlike walk.

Don't be a silent, "plastic" Christian. Talk about Jesus and live so that others can see him in you. Even if it's difficult, keep trying, as the four men did. You—yes, *you*—can bring people to Jesus.

Find the Missing Letters:
How to Help Your Friends

Write the letter that's missing from each set. Read the letters you wrote from left to right and write them in the blanks of the sentence.

A C D E F G H . . . . . . ___   O P Q S T U V . . . . . . ___

C D E F G H J . . . . . . ___   J K L M O P Q . . . . . . ___

D E F H I J K . . . . . . ___   Q R S U V W X . . . . . . ___

G I J K L M N . . . . . . ___   B C D F G H I . . . . . . ___

J K L N O P Q . . . . . . ___   P Q R S U V W . . . . . . ___

L M N P Q R S . . . . . . ___   H I K L M N O . . . . . . ___

A B C D F G H . . . . . . ___   R T U V W X Y . . . . . . ___

S T V W X Y Z . . . . . . ___   O P Q R T U V . . . . . . ___

The best help I can give my friends is to ___ ___ ___ ___ ___

___ ___ ___ ___   ___ ___   ___ ___ ___ ___ ___ .

37

A Tax Collector's Banquet

Introduction

Do not be proud, but be willing to associate with people of low position. Do not be conceited.

Romans 12:16

MORTIMER Monster said to his friend Herkimer, "Let's start a monster club." His friend agreed, and they sent invitations to all the monsters in town. When they came, Mortimer said, "Herkimer and I will decide who is good enough to join our club."

As the monsters filed by, Herkimer said, "That one can't join. He has purple skin with yellow dots."

"Neither can the next one," said Mortimer. "His nose is too big. And we can't let the one with dirty, old clothes join."

On and on they went, finding fault, until no one was left but Mortimer and Herkimer. "Hey, Herkimer, you're not fit to join my club, either," said Mortimer. "You have flat feet."

"Well, I'll just walk away on my flat feet and never come back," said Herkimer. So Mortimer Monster sat by himself in his clubhouse, lonely and miserable.

Being proud and conceited can limit our friendships. Some proud men did not like the friends Jesus chose. But Jesus had something to say to them.

THE FACTS, PLEASE!

1. *Tax collectors (publicans).* The Romans, who ruled over Palestine, made the Jews pay taxes to them. Roman officials sold the right to collect taxes to the highest bidder. Then that man hired local people to collect the taxes at booths along main roads. The greedy tax collectors charged much more money than the actual taxes and kept the extra for themselves. Most Jews hated them.

2. *Banquet.* A banquet in Bible times was a formal meal to celebrate a special occasion or to honor an important guest. People who were not invited would often watch the banquet from outside, looking through the windows or an open door. Each guest lay on a couch, leaning on his left elbow. His head faced the table, and he ate with a spoon or a piece of bread in his right hand.

3. *Pharisees.* There were about 6,000 Pharisees at the time of Jesus. They were Jews who were very strict about keeping the laws of God and the rules that

men had added to them. Many Pharisees were sincere, but Jesus said some of them did not practice what they preached. On the outside they appeared to be righteous. Inside, they were wicked. The Pharisees looked down on people they thought were not as good as they were.

Bible Story: A Humble Tax Collector and Haughty Pharisees
Matthew 9:9-13; Luke 5:27-32

Beside a main road near Capernaum, a man sat at a booth. Matthew, also called Levi, was collecting taxes. He looked down the road and saw Jesus coming toward him.

"Follow me," Jesus said to Matthew. This meant Jesus wanted Matthew to be one of his disciples. At once Matthew got up, left everything, and humbly followed Jesus.

Matthew, perhaps wanting everyone to know he had given up his business to follow Jesus, invited many friends to a banquet. Tax collectors and many other people came. Jesus and the other disciples were there, too. As they gathered around the tables and ate, some Pharisees watched them.

"Why does your teacher eat with tax collectors and sinners?" the Pharisees asked Jesus' disciples.

Jesus heard them. "People who are well don't need a doctor," he said. "Sick people do. I have not come to call the righteous, but sinners to repentance." The Pharisees thought they always did everything right and always pleased God. They didn't think they needed a Savior. With that attitude they would never be able to get Jesus' help.

This Is for You

The haughty Pharisees thought they were better than others. They did not want to associate with people who were different from themselves. But Jesus wants to be everyone's friend, including sinners. He is ready and willing to save them if they will receive him as Savior.

Jesus chose a tax collector, one whom many Jews hated, to be one of his disciples. Matthew became a faithful follower of Jesus. After Jesus went back to heaven, Matthew wrote the first book of the New Testament.

Lots of kids want to associate only with the "cool" crowd. They don't want anything to do with someone they call "dorky." That isn't Jesus' way, is it?

The kids that seem to be "nobodies" may turn out to be better friends than any of the "cool" kids. Treat others as you would like them to treat you. Look beyond their outward appearance to see what they are really like inside. And don't knock those who are different. Be their friend and helper.

A Coded Verse:
How to Treat Others Right

Using the code, fill in the blanks in the verse that tells what we should do when we're with others.

a	J	T	H	O	U
b	S	N	B	P	D
w	C	G	I	M	Y
d	K	E	R	A	
	1	2	3	4	5

" __ __ __ __   __ __ __ __ __ __ __   __ __
  b-1 a-2 a-4 b-4   a-1 a-5 b-5 c-2 c-3 b-2 c-2   b-3 c-5

__ __ __ __   __ __ __ __ __ __ __ __ __ __ __ ,
c-4 d-2 d-3 d-2   d-4 b-4 b-4 d-2 d-4 d-3 d-4 b-2 c-1 d-2 b-1

__ __ __   __ __ __ __   __   __ __ __ __ __
d-4 b-2 b-5   c-4 d-4 d-1 d-2   d-4   d-3 c-3 c-2 a-3 a-2

__ __ __ __ __ __ __ __." (John 7:24)
a-1 a-5 b-5 c-2 c-4 d-2 b-2 a-2

221

38

A Funeral
Turnabout

Introduction

For the wages of sin is death, but the gift of God is eternal life in Christ Jesus our Lord.

Romans 6:23

Long ago, a prisoner sat in a dark, dismal dungeon. He had been sentenced to death. The prisoner examined the heavy chains that shackled him. If he could break them, he had a plan for his escape. *If anyone can find a flaw in one of these links, I can,* he said to himself. *I am known as the best blacksmith in the country.*

Link by link, the prisoner looked for any weak spot. Then he found some marks that identified the chain as one he had made. *It's no use trying to break this chain,* he cried silently in dismay. *My boast is that no one can break a chain I made myself.*

All sinners are sentenced to death. Our sins are like chains that bind us tightly. We cannot escape by ourselves. The Bible story about a dead man teaches the one way of escape for every sinner.

The Facts, Please!

1. *Nain.* This city was located on a slope of the Hill of Moreh in Galilee, about five miles from Nazareth.
2. *Funeral (burial).* The burial of a dead body had to take place quickly in Bible times. The hot climate caused a body to decay very fast. Usually the body was washed and wrapped loosely in a linen cloth. Then it was carried to a burial place. Well-to-do people buried their dead relatives in a cave. Most others were buried in a shallow grave covered with stones. Mourners in the funeral procession were family, friends, and servants (if there were any). Wealthy people hired professional mourners to cry loudly or wail.
3. *Bier (coffin).* This was not like our coffins of today. It was usually just a wooden board on which a dead body was placed to be carried to a grave.
4. *Widow.* A woman whose husband has died is a widow. In Israel, when a man died, his widow did not inherit his property. If she did not have any children to take care of her, she was usually very poor.

Bible Story: A Dead Son Lives Again
Luke 7:11-17

On a trip through Galilee, Jesus and his disciples came to the town of Nain. A large crowd of people followed them. As they climbed the hill, they approached the town gate. There a funeral procession was starting down out of Nain.

Some men carried the bier, on which lay a young man. He was his mother's only son, and she was a widow. She wept as she walked along. Behind her came many people from the city who mourned with her.

When Jesus saw the widow, he felt very sorry for her. He knew she was a poor widow who had no one to care for her now. Tenderly, Jesus said, "Don't cry."

Then Jesus went up and touched the bier. The men who carried it stood still. Jesus said to the cold, motionless body, "Young man, I say to you, get up!"

At once, the young man sat up and began to talk. He was alive! Jesus gave him back to his mother. Imagine how the mother and son felt. They must have hugged and kissed each other for a long time and thanked Jesus again and again.

The funeral procession turned around and went back into the city. The people were filled with awe and praised God, saying, "A great prophet has appeared among us. God has come to help his people." The news about Jesus spread all over the land.

This Is for You

Because he is God, Jesus could raise the dead man. Only God has the power to raise the dead.

Death is separation. There are three kinds of death or separation.

One type of death is physical. When a person's physical body dies, his soul and spirit are separated from his body.

Another kind of death is spiritual death—being separated from God because of sin. "Your iniquities have separated you from your God" (Isaiah 59:2).

Worst of all is eternal death—being separated from God forever and living in hell. Every person is born a sinner, and we have all sinned. Sinners who never believe in Jesus as Savior will receive eternal death when they die physically.

Isn't it wonderful that we don't have to stay in the prison of sin, awaiting the death sentence? When we believe in Jesus, he breaks our chains of sin and sets us free. He gives us the gift of eternal life.

Have you received that gift? If not, would you like to do it? *See the last page of this book.*

Fill in the Blanks:
The Great Crossover

Put an X in the squares listed below, and use the remaining letters to fill in the blanks in the verse. After you have solved the puzzle, then look up the verse to check your answer.

Row A—Squares 2, 4, 5, 7, 9 Row D—Squares 2, 4, 5, 7, 8, 10

Row B—Squares 1, 6 Row E—Squares 1, 3, 4, 6, 9

Row C—Squares 3, 6, 8 Row F—Squares 1, 2, 4, 6, 8, 9

	1	2	3	4	5	6	7	8	9	10
A	H	D	E	P	T	A	S	R	O	S
B	D	B	E	L	I	X	E	V	E	S
C	E	T	W	E	R	V	N	F	A	L
D	L	C	I	D	P	F	T	H	E	N
E	M	D	N	L	E	X	A	T	W	H
F	H	G	L	Y	I	Z	F	Q	R	E

"I tell you the truth, whoever _____ my word and
                                        A

_____ him who sent me has _____
        B   C

_____ and will not be condemned; he has crossed
        D

over from _____ to _____." (John 5:24)
                E   F

39

Robbers, Rejecters, and a Rescuer

Introduction

Love your neighbor as yourself.

Mark 12:31

A PASTOR asked the richest woman in town to visit a poor old woman. "Find out what her needs are," the pastor said. He knew the rich woman could give the other woman anything she needed.

"All right. I guess it's my duty," the rich woman said. She found the old woman's apartment in a rundown building and was invited to come in.

The rich woman learned that there was no food in the dingy kitchen. "I'll see that the Welfare Board sends a worker to talk with you," she said.

"No, thank you," said the old woman. "I need no help."

Just then a woman who lived in the same building came

with food and clothing. "Thank you so much!" the old woman said.

"Wait a minute," the rich woman said. "You just refused my help, but you took hers. Why is that?"

"She's my neighbor," the poor woman replied. "I know she *wants* to help me, because I can feel her love."

The Facts, Please!

1. *Lawyer.* This was a man (a scribe) who knew and taught the Jewish law.
2. *Priests.* These men were descendants of Aaron, Moses' brother. Moses and Aaron were descendants of Jacob's son Levi. The priests were in charge of worship services in the temple. They prepared and offered sacrifices.
3. *Levites.* These men were also from the tribe of Levi. They helped the priests in the temple.
4. *Samaritans.* These Jewish people lived in Samaria, an area in Israel. When the Assyrians took most of the Samaritans away as captives, they left the poor people behind. These Jews married heathen people and worshiped their gods along with the true God. In Jesus' day, the Jewish people hated the Samaritans because they were not full-blooded Jews and did not worship God in Jerusalem.
5. *Inns.* Travelers in Bible times were in danger of bandits. They needed a safe place to stay at night. Also, they needed water and a place to lie down. In New Testament times, inns were built for travelers. They were simple, crude places where travelers could let their animals eat and sleep in safety, and where they could

lie down themselves on their own bedding. Innkeepers were in charge of the inns and sometimes provided food and care for the wounded.

Bible Story: Saving a Half-Dead Man
Luke 10:25-37

"Teacher, what must I do to inherit eternal life?" a lawyer asked Jesus, wanting to test him.

"What does God's Law say you must do?" Jesus asked him.

The lawyer answered, " 'Love the Lord your God with all your heart and with all your soul and with all your strength and with all your mind.' And it says, 'Love your neighbor as yourself.' "

"Correct," Jesus said. "Do this and you will live."

The lawyer, wanting to show he had done what was right, asked, "Who is my neighbor?"

Jesus answered with a story. "As a man walked from Jerusalem to Jericho, robbers grabbed him. They stripped him of his clothes, beat him, and ran away, leaving him half dead.

"A priest came along and saw the man, but he crossed to the other side of the road. Then a Levite also came along. He saw the man and crossed to the other side.

"Next, a Samaritan traveled that way, riding on his donkey. He saw the wounded man, took pity on him, and went to him. The Samaritan man poured wine on his wounds to disinfect them and poured oil to soothe the pain. Then he bandaged the cuts and bruises. He let the man ride the donkey he had been riding, and he took the man to an inn and cared for him.

"The next day, the Samaritan gave two silver coins to the

innkeeper. 'Take care of the man,' he said. 'I will return and pay you more for any extra expense you have.' "

Jesus asked the lawyer, "Which of these three men was a neighbor to the wounded man?"

"The one who was kind to him," the lawyer replied.

"Right," said Jesus. "You go and do the same."

This Is for You

The priest and the Levite were religious leaders. They knew the commandment, "Love your neighbor as yourself." Still, they did not even lift a finger to help the wounded man. Perhaps they didn't consider him to be their neighbor. Maybe they only did their good deeds when others could see them.

The Samaritan knew that Jewish people hated his people. Maybe some had even mistreated him. Yet he helped his wounded neighbor, who was probably a Jewish man.

Who is your neighbor—a person who lives near you or one of your good friends? Jesus showed by his story that a neighbor is anyone who is in need of help. "Love your neighbor as yourself"—no matter who the neighbor is.

Acrostic Puzzle:
The Good Neighbor

Fill in the blanks in the sentences with words from the Bible story. Then, in the puzzle, fill in #1 across and #2 down. Finish the remaining blanks in the puzzle.

1. The man who helped the wounded man was the

   _____.

2. This helper was a _____ to the hurt man.

3. A _____ asked Jesus how to have eternal life.

4. A temple helper, a _____ , passed by the hurt man.

5. We are to love _____ with all our being.

6. The man who questioned Jesus called him "_____."

7. _____ attacked the man, leaving him half dead.

8. The wounded man had been on his way to _____.

9. A _____ was the first man to pass by the hurt
   man.

2.

↓

1. __ __ __ __ __ __ __ __

      3. __ __ __ __ __ __

       4. __ __ __ __ __ __

        5. __ __ __

      6. __ __ __ __ __ __ __

       7. __ __ __ __ __ __ __

    8. __ __ __ __ __ __ __

       9. __ __ __ __ __ __

No Pigs' Pods for a Prodigal

Introduction

The Son of Man came to seek and to save what was lost.

Luke 19:10

Emily loved her beautiful, all-white cat. She liked his white fur so much that she named him simply *White Cat*. He followed her around as she played, and he slept at the foot of her bed during the night.

One evening White Cat did not come home. Emily and her mom looked in the yard for him. They called and called, but he never showed up. For several days Emily looked all over the neighborhood for her cat and asked if anyone had seen him.

A week passed. Again, when Emily woke up, she looked at the foot of her bed, just in case White Cat had come home. There he was! Emily took him in her arms and held him close. "You're home, White Cat! I've looked all over for you," she said.

Later, Emily's mom said that White Cat had meowed at the door during the night, and she had let him in.

Jesus told stories about a lost sheep, a lost coin, and a lost son. Were they found?

The Facts, Please!

1. *Inheritance.* According to Jewish law, when a man died, his property, possessions, and money were divided among his sons. The oldest son received twice as much as the other sons did.
2. *Pigs.* Why do pigs like to wallow in mud? Because they can't sweat. Some people call them dumb. Are they? No. Pigs are among the most intelligent animals. Today we can eat pork, but God listed pigs as one of the unclean animals that Jewish people were not to eat. For a Jewish man, taking care of pigs was very shameful.
3. *Pigs' pods.* Locust (carob) trees produced pods, or husks, which had sweet syrup inside. These pods were ground and fed to pigs and other livestock.
4. *Fattened calf.* This was a calf that had been penned up and fed very well. It was kept for a special occasion.

Bible Story: Home Again to Father
Luke 15:3-32

Jesus told three stories about lost things. This is the first story: A shepherd had 100 sheep, but one went away by itself. The shepherd left the 99 sheep and hunted for the lost one until he found it. In Jesus' second story, a woman lost one of her ten silver coins. She lit a candle, swept the house, and searched until she found it.

Here is Jesus' third story:

A man had two sons. The younger one said, "Father, give me my share of my inheritance." So the father divided his property between his sons. Taking the money from his part of the property, the younger son packed up his belongings and went on a long trip to a faraway country.

He lived a wild life and used up all his money. When a famine came to the land, he had no food. He could only find a job looking after pigs. How disgusting and shameful!

He watched the pigs eat the pods he fed them. "I wish I could fill my empty stomach with some of those," he said. But no one offered him any. Finally he came to his senses.

"The hired men who work for my father have plenty of food, and I am starving. I will go home," he decided. "I will say to my father, 'I have sinned against heaven and you. I am not worthy to be called your son. Make me like one of your hired men.' "

The young man started home. While he was still far off, his father saw him. The father ran to his son, threw his arms around him, and kissed him. Then the son said, "Father, I have sinned against heaven and you. I am not worthy to be called your son."

The father said to his servants, "Get the best robe and put it on him. Put a ring on his finger and sandals on his feet. Kill the fattened calf and cook it. We will have a feast. It seemed as if my son was dead, and now he is alive! He was lost, but now he is found."

This Is for You

The important truth Jesus taught about the three lost things is the love of the owners and the parent. The shepherd and the woman did not give up until they found what they had lost. Then they rejoiced. The father of the lost son anxiously waited for him to return. When he did, he hugged him tightly and had a feast in his honor.

Each of the three who lost something represents God. Our Father in heaven has showered us with good things. How have we treated him? "All have sinned," the Bible says. We have turned our backs on God. Our sins have separated us from him, and we are lost.

How does God treat us? "This is love: not that we loved God, but that he loved us and sent his Son as an atoning sacrifice for our sins" (1 John 4:10). Jesus said he came to seek and save what was lost. He loved us so much that he died on the cross, taking the punishment we deserve.

God anxiously waits for us to come to him. No matter how much we have sinned, he will forgive us and save us. "There is rejoicing in the presence of the angels of God over one sinner who repents" (Luke 15:10). Have you trusted Jesus to save you? If you are still lost, would you like to come to God now? *See the last page of this book.*

Letters and Numbers:
Good News for Sinners

Add or subtract numbers, then use the code to fill in the blanks. The first one is done for you. Write those letters again on the lines below the puzzle to complete the sentence.

1=D	2=V	3=M	4=G	5=N	6=O	7=L
8=T	9=E	10=S	11=A	12=W	13=H	14=C

```
  2    8    5    3    3    6    3    5    9    6    8
 +2   -2   -4   +4   +3   -4   +6   +5   -1   +7   +1
 ___  ___  ___  ___  ___  ___  ___  ___  ___  ___  ___
  4
 ___  ___  ___  ___  ___  ___  ___  ___  ___  ___  ___
  G
```

```
  5    4    4   10    5    8    1    5    2    9    9
 +2   +2   +6   -2   +6   -3   +0   +7   +7   -2   +5
 ___  ___  ___  ___  ___  ___  ___  ___  ___  ___  ___

 ___  ___  ___  ___  ___  ___  ___  ___  ___  ___  ___
```

```
  4    6   12    7    5   10    6    2    5    2    7    6
 +2   -3   -3   +3   +3   +3   +3   +1   +8   +4   -4   +3
 ___  ___  ___  ___  ___  ___  ___  ___  ___  ___  ___  ___

 ___  ___  ___  ___  ___  ___  ___  ___  ___  ___  ___  ___
```

G __ __   __ __ __ __ __   __ __ __   __ __ __ __

__ __ __   __ __ __ __ __ __ __   __ __ __ __

__ __ __ __.

41

Donkeys, Hosannas, and Palm Branches

Introduction

O Lord, our Lord, how majestic is your name in all the earth! You have set your glory above the heavens. From the lips of children and infants you have ordained praise.

Psalm 8:1-2

Praise and Petition

Two angels left from heaven's gates to gather up the prayers;
They carried golden baskets and descended golden stairs.
As they would hear the people pray from all the earth around,
They'd fill their baskets to the top and then be heaven bound.
One gathered up petitions, and he soon could travel back;
The other sought for praises, but he found there was a lack.
And so we learn a lesson true: of prayers that people raise,
Petitions are abounding, but there's very little praise.

This poem is based on an old legend. Angels don't really gather prayers in baskets. But the truth is there. When we petition God, we ask him to give *us* something. When we praise him, we give *him* something. Which do we do most often?

The Facts, Please!

1. *A king's transportation.* In Bible times, horses were used to pull chariots, and they carried soldiers into battle. A king often rode a prancing horse into a city to celebrate a victory in battle. When he rode a donkey, it usually meant he was coming peacefully. Solomon rode a donkey when he was crowned as king of Israel.
2. *Hosanna.* This word means, "Save us, please!" It was first used as a prayer for help. By the time Jesus was on earth, it had come to be used as a cry of joy or a shout of victory.
3. *Palm leaves.* The date palm has long, leathery leaves on branches that are six to eight feet long. It was an ancient custom to pluck off palm branches and wave them as a welcome to a king. This was a symbol of victory.
4. *Prophecy.* When a prophet tells something that will happen in the future, it is called a prophecy. Hundreds of years before Jesus was born, a prophet wrote, "Shout, Daughter of Jerusalem! See, your king comes to you, righteous and having salvation, gentle and riding on a donkey, on a colt, the foal of a donkey" (Zechariah 9:9). The New Testament tells about a time in Jesus' life when this prophecy came true.

Bible Story: Make Way for the King!
Matthew 21:1-17; Mark 11:1-10; Luke 19:28-40; John 12:12-19

As Jesus walked with his disciples toward Jerusalem, he told two of them, "Go to the village ahead of us. As you enter it, you will see a colt tied there. It will be a young colt on which no one has ever ridden. Untie it and bring it to me. If someone asks what you are doing, tell him the Lord needs it and will return it soon."

The two disciples found the colt in the street, tied at a doorway. As they started to untie it, some people standing there asked, "Why are you doing that?" The disciples told them what Jesus had said, and the people let them have the donkey.

The disciples put their coats on the donkey's back. Jesus climbed on and rode toward Jerusalem. Some people who had seen Jesus heal the sick and raise the dead followed him. A great crowd of Jews had come to Jerusalem for the Feast of the Passover. Many of them joined the procession.

People threw their coats on the road in front of Jesus. Others cut down tree branches and spread them in his path. They waved palm branches and shouted joyfully, "Hosanna! Blessed is he who comes in the name of the Lord! Blessed is the coming kingdom of our father David! Hosanna in the highest!"

Jesus went into the temple area. Blind and lame people came to him, and he healed them. Children shouted, "Hosanna!"

The priests and teachers of the law asked Jesus, "Do you hear what they are saying?"

"Yes," replied Jesus. "Have you never heard anyone read these words: 'From the lips of children and infants you have received praise'?"

This Is for You

Many people praised Jesus that day. Some were excited and joyful, because they thought Jesus had come to be their king. They expected him to lead them to defeat their Roman rulers. Later, when Jesus was on trial, some of those same people were probably with the crowd that shouted, "Crucify him!"

Other people truly loved Jesus, and their praise came from their heart. Jesus especially liked the praise of the honest and sincere children.

Jesus wants us to ask him for the things we need. He loves to shower us with good things. But it must make him sad when we keep asking for things and then don't praise him much at all.

Don't forget to praise Jesus every day. How can you praise him? Tell him that you praise and worship him as King of kings. And let him know that you want him to be your Savior and Lord. Thank him for dying on the cross for your sins. Thank him for answered prayers and for all he has done for you. You can be sure he will hear your praise. He has a special delight in the praise of children.

Cross Out Letters and Fill in Blanks:
Who Should Praise the Lord?

The last verse in the book of Psalms answers this question. To find out what it says, cross out the letters *C, F, J, K, M,* and *Q* in the boxes below. Fill in the blanks in the verse with the remaining letters in the order they are written (going from left to right).

L	K	F	E	C	T	Q	E	V	M
J	E	R	C	Y	M	T	H	F	Q
I	N	K	F	G	T	C	F	H	A
T	M	Q	H	J	A	S	B	F	R
Q	E	C	F	K	A	T	M	H	P
J	R	A	M	I	C	S	J	E	T
H	K	E	C	L	M	O	F	R	D

—— —— —— —— —— —— —— —— —— —— —— ——

—— —— —— —— —— —— —— —— —— —— ——

—— —— —— —— —— —— —— —— —— —— —— —— ——.

(Psalm 150:6)

Does this include you? _____

42

The Fruitless Fig Tree

Introduction

He is like a tree planted by streams of water, which yields its fruit in season and whose leaf does not wither. Whatever he does prospers. Not so the wicked! They are like chaff that the wind blows away.

Psalm 1:3-4

A MAN was walking on his way to a Halloween party dressed like a devil. Before he arrived, it began to rain hard, so he dashed inside the nearest open building. It turned out to be a church where a revival meeting was going on.

As soon as the people saw the man in his devil costume, they rushed to get out through the doors and windows. One woman caught her dress on the handle of a seat and couldn't get loose. The man in the costume came nearer, and she begged him, "Please, Mr. Satan, don't hurt me! I've been a member of this church for 20 years, but I've really been on your side all the time!"

The woman in this joke was a hypocrite—a person who pretends to be what she is not. Jesus came across a tree one day. It was like a hypocrite!

The Facts, Please!

1. *Fig tree.* These fig-producing trees were valued for their fruit and their shade. In the right kind of soil, they could grow to be 30 feet tall. The broad leaves of a fig tree were large enough to be a covering for Adam and Eve. If a fig tree had leaves, that usually meant it also had fruit.
2. *Figs.* This delicious fruit was a favorite in Bible times. It was eaten fresh or pressed into cakes and preserved by drying.
3. *Fruit of the Spirit.* A Christian is like a good, fruitful tree, planted by streams of water. The Holy Spirit produces fruit on this tree. The fruit is named in Galatians 5:22-23: "The fruit of the Spirit is love, joy, peace, patience, kindness, goodness, faithfulness, gentleness, and self-control."
4. *Hypocrisy.* Hypocrites, who pretend to be what they're not, are showing hypocrisy.

Bible Story: Nothing But Leaves
Mark 11:12-14, 20-21

Jesus and his disciples left Bethany one morning to go to Jerusalem. As they walked along, Jesus saw a fig tree in the distance. At that time of year, if a tree had leaves, that usually meant it also had fruit. But when Jesus got up close, he found nothing but leaves.

Jesus spoke to the tree, "May no one ever eat fruit from you again." Jesus' disciples heard what he said.

The next day, as they passed by the tree again, they saw that the tree was withered from the roots. "Look, Master!" Peter said. "The tree you cursed is withered away." That tree would never bear leaves or fruit again.

Through this incident, Jesus gave an object lesson to the disciples about hypocrisy. The fig tree with its leaves was saying, "I have fruit." But it had no fruit. It was saying one thing and doing another. It was like a hypocrite.

When Jesus was on earth, most of the Israelites claimed to know God, but they rejected Jesus. He told them he was the Son of God, and they saw him perform miracles. Still they would not believe in him. They even thought they were better than he was!

The fig tree may represent Israel. However, it can also stand for any person who professes to know Christ as Savior and Lord but is just pretending.

This Is for You

Many people claim to be Christians. They talk like Christians, and they try to act like Christians. All they have in their lives, though, is leaves. They have no fruit. Not all Christians have the same amount of fruit, but all who are genuine will have some fruit.

When Jesus saves us from our sins, the Holy Spirit helps us to be like Jesus. And he helps us have love, joy, and peace, no matter what happens. When others are unkind to us, he helps us show patience, kindness, and goodness to them. In difficult times, he develops in us faithfulness, gentleness, and self-control. That is being like Jesus. It is also bearing fruit.

A tree has sap that runs through its trunk and branches, and it develops the fruit. The Holy Spirit is like that. If you let him take charge, he will bear the fruit in you.

This doesn't happen all at once. Bearing fruit takes time. Each day, read your Bible and pray. Ask the Holy Spirit to make you what you ought to be that very day. Then your "tree" will have more than leaves. It will bear fruit—a big crop of it!

Fill in the Blanks:
A Good Tree Bears Fruit

Look up Luke 6:43-45, and fill in the blanks.

"No good _____ bears bad _____ , nor does a bad _____ bear good _____. Each _____ is recognized by its own _____. People do not pick _____ from _____ , or _____ from _____. The good _____ brings good _____ out of the good stored up in his _____ , and the evil _____ brings evil _____ out of the evil stored up in his _____. For out of the overflow of his _____ his _____ speaks." (Luke 6:43-45)

43

A Whip, a Crown of Thorns, and a Purple Robe

Introduction

**"What shall I do, then, with Jesus who is called Christ?"
Pilate asked. They all answered, "Crucify him!"**

Matthew 27:22

A GROUP of high school students in Detroit skipped school and went to a rock concert. They thought they got away with it. The next morning the *Detroit News* carried a color photo of the concert on the front page. In it, as plain as could be, were the high school students who had cut classes.

The school principal spotted their pictures and called the students to his office. There was nothing they could say except, "We are guilty."

All of us are guilty of sin. Someone was born into this world and lived for 33 years without sinning even once. He was never guilty of a bad thought, word, or deed. Yet he stood in court one day and witnesses declared, "He is guilty!"

The Facts, Please!

1. *Crown of thorns.* A crown is worn to show a person's authority or place of high honor. The Roman soldiers put a crown of thorns on Jesus' head to mock him. We do not know what kind of thorns they were. They may have been from a plant in the buckthorn family, whose thorns have both curved and straight spines.
2. *Scourges.* These were whips made of leather straps attached to a handle. Bits of sharp metal or bone in the straps cut into a person's flesh and caused severe pain.
3. *Purple robe.* Usually a robe was an outer garment worn over other clothes. Kings and wealthy people wore purple robes.
4. *Sanhedrin.* This was a group of 71 Jews who were experts in Jewish law. This group, also called "the council," was like a Jewish supreme court. The final word, though, came from the Romans, who ruled over the land in those days.

Bible Story: An Innocent Man Is Declared Guilty
Matthew 26:57-68; 27:11-31; Mark 14:53-65; 15:1-20

Jesus and 11 disciples entered the Garden of Gethsemane one night. Jesus knew he would die the next day. He knelt down and prayed, "Father, if you are willing, take this cup from me; yet not my will but yours be done." His agony was so great that his sweat poured out like drops of blood falling to the ground. He must have dreaded taking the sins of the world on himself. He also undoubtedly dreaded the pain he knew he would have to bear.

After praying three times, Jesus woke his disciples, who had fallen asleep. Suddenly, a crowd marched up, led by one of Jesus' own disciples, Judas. They carried torches, swords, and clubs. Judas kissed Jesus, and the men seized him.

Jesus went willingly with his captors. They put him on trial before the high priest and the Sanhedrin. They found two men who testified against Jesus, telling lies.

When Jesus said he was the Christ, the high priest tore his robes. "This man is telling us that he is God. That's blasphemy," he said. "What do you think?"

"He is worthy of death!" everyone cried. They sent Jesus to Pilate, the Roman ruler, who had the power to order his death. Pilate and another ruler, Herod, could find no fault in Jesus. Still, the Jewish people cried, "Crucify him!" Pilate didn't want trouble with the Jews, so he agreed.

Jesus endured terrible things. The soldiers whipped him on his bare back. They twisted a crown of thorns and pressed it on his head. They put a purple robe on him and made fun of him.

Jesus, the Lord of the universe, did not say a word. He allowed such cruelties because of his love for a wicked world—for us. He was innocent, yet the soldiers took him out to crucify him.

This Is for You

At the time when Jesus was arrested, he had a question for those who came to capture him in the garden. He said, "Don't you think I can call on my Father and ask him to send thousands of angels to help me?" Jesus didn't ask for that, though. He had come into the world to die for our sins, so he willingly went to be tried and crucified.

Guilty! We don't like to hear that word. Sometimes it is true. We do wrong and try to hide it. Then someone finds out and says, "You are guilty." But there is something worse: being accused of guilt when we are innocent. That's the way it was with Jesus.

All people are guilty of sin and deserve to die. Jesus, God's Son, never sinned, yet he loved us so much that he let people say he was guilty. The innocent one took the punishment for all the guilty ones.

Have you thanked Jesus for taking your place and your punishment? The first way to thank him is to receive him as your Savior. Have you done that? If not, here is another opportunity to do so. *See the last page of this book.*

Word Search:
Jesus' Unfair Capture and Trial

Find and circle the words from the story that are listed. You can go up, down, and across, backward, and diagonally.

```
S   E   I   L   S   D   E   A   T   H   D
S   G   E   I   W   O   R   D   L   E   S
A   E   N   A   M   E   S   H   T   E   G
N   N   G   P   R   I   E   S   T   N   D
H   G   E   B   O   R   P   U   E   E   J
E   D   A   C   L   W   A   S   L   R   U
D   T   O   R   S   O   T   E   L   E   D
R   A   L   O   D   R   V   J   S   H   A
I   E   L   W   L   E   L   E   B   T   S
N   W   I   N   N   B   N   A   U   A   W
I   S   W   D   I   V   C   O   L   F   E
T   R   I   A   L   K   E   L   C   T   J
```

BACK	DEATH	GARDEN	JUDAS	ROBE	TRIAL
BLOOD	DIE	GETHSEMANE	LIES	SANHEDRIN	TWO
CLUBS	ELEVEN	JESUS	LOVE	SIN	WILL
CROWN	FATHER	JEWS	PRIEST	SWEAT	WORD

Spikes and Crosses on Skull Hill

Introduction

It was not with perishable things such as silver or gold that you were redeemed . . . but with the precious blood of Christ.

1 Peter 1:18-19

Once there were two boys in a town in Scotland who were great friends. When they grew up, one became an outstanding judge. The other one was caught committing a terrible crime. When the criminal came into court, he saw that the judge was his boyhood friend.

Oh, he thought, *what luck! I'm sure he'll go easy on me.*

The judge heard the case and then asked an assistant to bring the law book containing the penalties for crimes. "There are two penalties for your crime," the judge told the criminal. "One is a small fine, and the other is a large fine."

The prisoner hoped for the small fine, but the judge gave him the large one. The prisoner hung his head in despair. "George, my old friend," the judge said, "I have judged you fairly. Now I will save you as a friend. I myself will pay every cent of your penalty. You are a free man."

As you read the story of Jesus' crucifixion, remember that he hung on the cross to pay your penalty for your sins.

The Facts, Please!

1. *Crucifixion.* This was a method for putting someone to death. The person was placed on a wooden cross. Many nations, including the Romans, chose this kind of torturous death for criminals. It was a shameful, painfully slow death.
2. *Cross.* A wooden crosspiece, fastened to an upright stake, formed a cross. Crosses were in several shapes. Jesus' cross was probably one in which the stake extended above the crosspiece for a short distance.
3. *Spikes.* The nails used in crucifixion had to be large spikes that could hold the weight of a person. In 1968 the remains of a victim of crucifixion were found in the Holy Land. A seven-inch spike still pierced his anklebone, which was attached to a fragment of his cross.
4. *Skull Hill.* Jesus was crucified on a hill called *Golgotha*, which means "skull." Another name with the same meaning is *Calvary.* No one knows exactly where this hill is. The Bible says it was outside Jerusalem. There is a hill outside the city that is shaped like a skull.
5. *Redeemer.* This is a person who pays a ransom for

another person. For example, a redeemer might pay the price to set a slave free.

Bible Story: The Redeemer Dies Between Two Robbers
Luke 23:26-49; John 19:16-37

After Jesus' trial, the soldiers placed a cross on Jesus' bleeding shoulders and led him away to be crucified. Because of all the torture and beating that Jesus had gone through, he was too weak to carry the cross. When he fell down, the soldiers seized a man named Simon to carry the cross. A crowd of people followed Jesus, many of them weeping.

When they came to the hill of Golgotha, the soldiers nailed Jesus to his cross. Then they lifted it up, and he hung there. "Father, forgive them," Jesus prayed, "for they don't know what they are doing." It was nine o'clock in the morning.

The people stood watching Jesus. Some of the rulers made fun of him, saying, "He saved others. Let him save himself if he is the Christ." The soldiers mocked him also.

Two criminals were crucified along with Jesus, one on either side of him. One of the men made fun of Jesus by saying, "If you are the Christ, save yourself and us." Jesus could have come down from the cross, but he didn't. He was there to take the punishment for our sins, and he finished what he came to do.

The other criminal said, "We are being punished for our crimes, but this man has done nothing wrong." Then he said, "Jesus, remember me when you come into your kingdom."

Jesus replied, "Today you will be with me in paradise."

Even the sun hid its face, and darkness came over the city right at noon. At three o'clock, after six long hours, Jesus cried, "It is finished!" He gave his spirit into the hands of his Father, and he died.

This Is For You

Who caused Jesus to be crucified? Many people did. Judas, one of Jesus' disciples, led Jesus' enemies to where he was. These Jewish enemies brought Jesus into court and accused him of doing wrong. The high priest said Jesus was worthy of death. Pilate handed him over to the crowd that said, "Crucify him!" The Roman soldiers drove the spikes into his hands and feet.

Yes, all of these people had a part in causing Jesus' death. But so did you and I. We caused him to be nailed to the cross, because it was *our sins* that put him there. "Christ died for our sins according to the Scriptures" (1 Corinthians 15:3).

All of us have done wrong in God's sight. We deserve to be punished. The penalty for our sins is eternal separation from God—eternity in hell. Jesus loved us so much that he didn't want us to be punished. He redeemed us by paying the price of our ransom. Now all who receive Jesus as Savior are set free from paying the penalty of sin.

Coded Words:
Two Robbers and a Savior

Three words beginning with *R* describe what the three men on the crosses did that day. Two words beginning

with *H* tell where they went as a result of what they did. Using the code, fill in the blanks.

1	2	3	4	5	6	7	8	9	10	11	12	13
M	J	R	E	D	L	C	I	V	H	T	A	N

1. When Jesus died on the cross for our sins, he became our

__ __ __ __ __ __ __ __.
 3 4 5 4 4 1 4 3

2. The robber who mocked Jesus was a

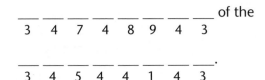

__ __ __ __ __ __ __ __ of the
 3 4 2 4 7 11 4 3

__ __ __ __ __ __ __ __.
 3 4 5 4 4 1 4 3

3. The robber who believed in Jesus was a

__ __ __ __ __ __ __ __ of the
 3 4 7 4 8 9 4 3

__ __ __ __ __ __ __ __.
 3 4 5 4 4 1 4 3

4. The __ __ __ __ __ __ __ __ went to __ __ __ __.
         3 4 2 4 7 11 4 3   10 4 6 6

5. The __ __ __ __ __ __ __ __ went to
         3 4 7 4 8 9 4 3

__ __ __ __ __ __.
10 4 12 9 4 13

45

Escape from a Cocoon and a Sealed Tomb

Introduction

Jesus said to her, "I am the resurrection and the life. He who believes in me will live, even though he dies."

John 11:25

A CATERPILLAR begins life as a tiny egg. Its mother lays it on or near the plant it will later use for its food. The egg hatches into a tiny caterpillar with an enormous appetite. It eats plant food and grows very rapidly.

Soon the caterpillar outgrows its skin, which splits open. With its new elastic skin, it crawls out in a process called *molting*. It molts four or five times, until it is full-grown.

After the last molt, the caterpillar is covered with an oddly shaped hard skin, called a *cocoon*. At that point the caterpillar has no eyes, mouth, antennae, or legs. Inside its case, big changes take place. The body becomes a soft, creamy liquid. Wings, legs, and other body parts slowly form. After a while, the cocoon splits.

A butterfly emerges, weak and covered with moisture. It hangs upside down, waving its wings until they spread out and harden. Before long, the beautiful creature flies into the air.

One time Jesus was inside something we might call a "cocoon." But he was able to get out only because of his supernatural power as God's only Son.

The Facts, Please!

1. *Tombs and tombstones.* In Bible times, usually only well-to-do people were buried in tombs, which were caves or chambers dug out of rock. A man named Joseph from the town of Arimathea placed Jesus' body in a new tomb that he had cut out of a rock. Nicodemus went with him. He rolled a heavy, round tombstone across the entrance.

2. *Grave clothes.* Jesus' body was covered with spices and wrapped in linen strips that were wound around his body like a cocoon. A separate cloth was on his head.

3. *Guards.* Roman soldiers guarded the tomb of Jesus night and day. To sleep while posted as a guard meant death for a Roman soldier. Yet notice in the story the lie they told about Jesus' body.

Bible Story: Jesus Lives Again
Matthew 27:57-66; 28:1-15; John 19:38-42; 20:1-23

With Pilate's permission, Joseph and Nicodemus took Jesus' body for burial. Nicodemus brought 75 pounds of spices with him. The two men covered Jesus' body with the spices and wrapped him in strips of linen cloth. They laid his body in Joseph's new tomb and rolled the stone over the entrance.

The next day the chief priests and Pharisees said to Pilate, "Sir, we heard Jesus say he would rise again in three days. Give the order for the tomb to be made secure. Then Jesus' disciples can't steal his body and say he rose again."

Pilate said, "Make the tomb as secure as you can." So they put a seal on the stone and posted a guard to watch the tomb.

Early on the first day of the week, all was quiet at the tomb. Suddenly there was an earthquake, and an angel in dazzling white clothes appeared! He rolled away the stone and sat on it. The frightened guards fell down like dead men.

Later, the guards told the chief priests what had happened. The priests gave the guards a large amount of money to lie. "Say that the disciples stole the body while you slept," they said. "If the governor hears this, we will see that he doesn't give you any trouble." The guards took the money and did what they were told.

Just after sunrise, three women came to the tomb, bringing more spices for Jesus' body. When they saw the angel, they were very frightened.

"Don't be afraid," the angel said. "Jesus is not here. He is alive. Go and tell his disciples."

The women hurried to share the good news.

When they heard it, Peter and John ran to the tomb. John looked in, but Peter went on inside. Then John came in. They both saw the linen strips lying there. They saw the head cloth also, folded by itself. John believed then that Jesus had truly come alive.

Later that day, the disciples met in a locked room. All at once, Jesus stood there with them. He showed them the nail scars in his hands and his feet. With great joy, they welcomed their Lord. Truly, he was alive!

This Is for You

Jesus' "cocoon" was not torn apart or split. He came right out of the strips of cloth without disturbing them. He entered a room with locked doors. Yet he was not a ghost. We know he had a real body, for he ate some food, and the disciples could touch him.

A caterpillar's body is changed into a beautiful butterfly that emerges from its cocoon. It is not earthbound; it can fly. Jesus came out of the tomb with a new, heavenly body.

All who belong to Jesus will be changed someday when Jesus comes back again. Those who are dead and in the grave will come alive, with their bodies changed to new ones. Those who are alive will also be changed so their new bodies are like the body Jesus had when he came out of the tomb.

"He who believes in me will live, even though he dies," Jesus said. If Jesus is your Savior, you will have a new, perfect body to enjoy in heaven. Isn't that super good news?

Find the Verses and Fill the Blanks:
The Angel's Message

When the women came to the tomb, expecting to see Jesus' dead body, the angel had a special message for them. Find each Bible verse, count to the word given, and write it in the blanks.

Verse	Word	↓
John 2:19	#14	__ __ __ __ __
Acts 3:15	#6	__ __ __ __
Luke 24:39	#17	__ __ __ __ __
1 Corinthians 6:14	#10	__ __ __ __
Acts 2:32	#3	__ __ __ __ __ __
Psalm 49:15	#4	__ __ __ __ __ __
Acts 1:3	#2	__ __ __
1 Corinthians 15:42	#15	__ __ __ __
1 Corinthians 15:20	#4	__ __ __ __ __ __
2 Corinthians 4:14	#3	__ __ __ __

Now read down from the arrow to discover the angel's message. Then read the whole message in Matthew 28:6.

267

46

Wind, Fire, Tongues, and the Spirit

Introduction

[Jesus said,] "You will receive power when the Holy Spirit comes on you; and you will be my witnesses in Jerusalem, and in all Judea and Samaria, and to the ends of the earth."

Acts 1:8

SUPPOSE you are walking with your dad down a dark road at night. It is very difficult to see where to walk. Then a neighbor comes along with a flashlight. He hands it to you, and you try to turn it on. Nothing happens.

"Hey, what kind of flashlight is this?" you ask. "I can't get the light to come on."

"Oh, I forgot to put batteries in it," your neighbor says.

Batteries give a flashlight the power to shine. Without power, there is no light.

Jesus wants you to let your light shine. If you do that, people will be able to "see your good deeds and praise your Father in heaven" (Matthew 5:16). But without power, your light for Jesus will not shine. The only power that can make your light shine is the Holy Spirit. How can you have his power? Read on.

The Facts, Please!

1. *The Holy Spirit.* The Holy Spirit is invisible, yet he is a real Person. He is one of the three Persons that make up our one God. In Old Testament times the Holy Spirit gave power to individuals at certain times. He gave people power for doing special jobs for him. Now the Holy Spirit always lives inside believers. He is our Helper at all times.

2. *Fire.* The tongues (flames) of fire that sat on each person in this story were not actual fire. They looked like fire. Do you remember that fire in the Bible often shows that God is present? The tongues of fire showed that the Holy Spirit had come to earth to stay.

3. *Violent wind.* People heard the sound of a violent wind blowing. It was another sign that the Holy Spirit had come. We cannot see wind, but a violent wind certainly shows us its power. We cannot see the Holy Spirit, but he shows us his power in many ways.

4. *Tongues.* These were actual languages, spoken by people who had never known them before. People from many countries were in Jerusalem for the Day of Pentecost. Each person there could hear and

understand the Gospel message about Jesus in his own language.

Bible Story: Good-Bye, Jesus; Welcome, Holy Spirit
Acts 1:1-15; 2:1-14, 22-24, 36-41

Forty days passed after Jesus came back to life. Many of his followers saw him. One day he said to his disciples, "Stay in Jerusalem until you have received power from on high."

On the 40th day, Jesus led his disciples to the Mount of Olives. He said, "You will receive power when the Holy Spirit comes upon you, and you will be my witnesses everywhere."

As Jesus lifted up his hands and blessed the disciples, he began to rise from the earth. Higher, higher, higher he went, until a cloud hid him from sight. The disciples kept staring into the sky. Suddenly two men in white clothing stood beside them.

"Why do you men stand here looking into the sky?" they asked. "This same Jesus who went away will come again."

The disciples went to Jerusalem, as Jesus had told them to do. Ten days after Jesus left, about 120 followers of Jesus were in an upstairs room together. Suddenly they heard a sound like the blowing of a violent windstorm. It came from the skies above them and filled the house. What looked like tongues of fire divided and rested on each person. The people began to speak in languages they had not known before. They were able to do that because the Holy Spirit had come to live inside them.

People in the city heard the sound of the wind. A great crowd ran to the place where the disciples were. The power of the Holy Spirit made the disciples courageous and strong. Eagerly, they continued to speak in other languages. The amazed people said, "How can this be? These people from Galilee speak in the languages of many lands."

Then Peter preached a powerful message about Jesus to the crowd. When he finished, over 3,000 people believed in Jesus.

This Is for You

When we trust Jesus as Savior, the Holy Spirit comes to live inside us. We don't need to hear a wind or see flames of fire. We know the Holy Spirit is there, because the Bible says he is.

If you are a Christian, Jesus wants you to let your light shine by telling others about him. Do you find that hard to do? Then remember the flashlight. It needs battery power to shine.

You have the power of the Holy Spirit to help you witness. When you let him take charge, he will give you the power you need to be courageous and strong.

Pray every day for the Holy Spirit to help you witness. Then look for opportunities to tell others the good news of salvation. Don't be bashful or afraid. Speak up! You'll be surprised how much easier it becomes after a while. Soon you may win someone to Jesus. Wouldn't that be fantastic?

Crossword Puzzle:
Be a Witness

To write a statement about witnessing, fill in the puzzle, then write the words in the blanks of the statement on the next page.

Down

1. First name of our Helper

2. Second name of our Helper

3. The name of our Savior

4. Opposite of *take*

9. Allow

Across

5. Might; force

6. Opposite of *won't*

7. Belonging to you

8. Glow

9. Opposite of *dark*

10. Opposite of *from*

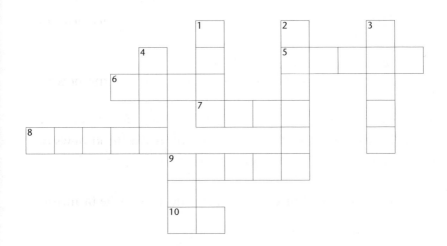

SEVEN DUCKS IN DIRTY WATER

The _____ _____ _____ _____
    (1 down)   (2 down)   (6 across)   (4 down)

you _____ _____ _____ _____
    (5 across)   (10 across)   (9 down)   (7 across)

_____ _____ for _____.
   (9 across)   (8 across)   (3 down)

47

A Beggar at the Gate and Trouble for Peter and John

Introduction

Peter and John replied, "Judge for yourselves whether it is right in God's sight to obey you rather than God. For we cannot help speaking about what we have seen and heard."

Acts 4:19-20

Look at my shirt, Grandma," said three-year-old Christopher. "I've got a picture of a tiger on it."

"That's not a tiger," said Grandma. "It's a lion. See the letters underneath? They are L-I-O-N. That spells 'lion.' "

"No. The letters are A-B-C-D, and that spells 'tiger,' " Christopher insisted. "I have a tiger on my shirt!"

Christopher couldn't spell yet, but he didn't believe his grandma.

Many Jewish rulers and priests did not believe what the

disciples said about Jesus. Those leaders didn't think that Jesus was the Son of God. So they insisted the disciples were lying when they said he arose from the dead. They knew the disciples performed miracles in the name of Jesus. Still they refused to believe the truth. See what the disciples did in this story.

The Facts, Please!

1. *Beggars.* The New Testament tells about people who begged for a living because they were sick or handicapped in some way. They usually begged at the doors of rich people, by the side of a road, or in front of a gate at the temple. People thought that giving to beggars was a good way to gain God's favor. That's why a temple gate was a good place to beg.

2. *Beautiful Gate.* This was a magnificent entrance into one of the courts in Herod's Temple. Made of solid bronze, it was probably about 75 feet high.

3. *Solomon's Colonnade.* A colonnade is a passageway with columns that support a roof. This one was on the east side of the temple that Herod built. It was called by Solomon's name, but his temple had been destroyed long before.

4. *Sadducees.* Most of the high priests and other Jewish rulers in the New Testament were Sadducees. Many merchants and rich people were Sadducees, too. They did not believe in the resurrection of the dead or eternal life for the soul.

Bible Story: A Leaping Lame Man and Two Brave Disciples
Acts 3:1-24; 4:1-23, 31; 5:17–42

Peter and John went to the temple one afternoon for prayer. A lame beggar sat every day at the Beautiful Gate of the temple. He had not walked in all his 40 years. When they passed him, the beggar pleaded, "Please give me some money."

Peter said, "Look at us!" The man looked up, expecting some money. "I have no silver and gold," Peter said. "But what I have I give you. In the name of Jesus Christ, get up and walk." Peter took the man's hand and helped him up. Instantly, his feet and anklebones became strong.

Leaping and walking, the man went into the temple court with Peter and John. "Praise God! Praise God!" he cried.

People watched him, amazed. "The lame man who sat at the Beautiful Gate is walking!" they said. They rushed to Solomon's Colonnade, where the man held tightly to Peter and John.

"Why are you surprised?" Peter asked. "This was done in the power of Jesus Christ, the one you crucified." Peter urged the people to believe in Jesus as their Savior, and many did believe.

The priests and Sadducees came to Peter and John. They were very upset that Peter was preaching about Jesus and life after death. They seized Peter and John and put them in jail.

The next day the priests and rulers called for a council meeting. They had Peter and John brought to them. "By what power or in whose name have you done this?" they asked.

Filled with the power of the Holy Spirit, Peter said, "We are being questioned because we did an act of kindness to a lame man. It is by the name of Jesus Christ that this man was healed." Then Peter preached the Good News of salvation to them.

"Never speak or teach in the name of Jesus again," the rulers sternly commanded the two disciples.

"We cannot help but speak," Peter said. When they were released, Peter and John kept right on preaching about Jesus.

This Is for You

The Sadducees and other rulers heard Jesus preach. They saw him perform miracles. They heard he had risen from the dead. But they refused to believe the truth. They insisted on saying that Jesus was not God's Son and that he did not come alive.

Have you been told not to take your Bible to school or pray in the lunchroom? Has a teacher scolded you for talking about Jesus? Some people claim these things violate the separation of church and state, as in the First Amendment of the Constitution.

They, too, believe a lie. The First Amendment was written to keep the state from interfering with the church. It was not the other way around. The founders of our country came here to get away from governments that ruled the church.

When the disciples were told not to preach about Jesus, they told the leaders, "We must obey God rather than you!"

Will you take a stand for Jesus, too? Will you pray before lunch and let your friends know what you've been reading in the Bible?

Don't follow those who believe a lie. Believe the truth and proudly tell it wherever you can.

Fill in the Blanks:
Why Were Jesus' Disciples Brave?

After preaching about Jesus, the disciples were put in jail again. An angel came at night, opened the doors, and let them out. The Jewish leaders had them beaten and again told them not to preach about Jesus. What did the disciples do? Write the words from the Word List in the correct blanks in the verse. Then unscramble the letters in the circles and use them to answer the question.

Word List

temple   news   never   Jesus   day   teaching   good   house

Day after ___ ___ ◯ , in the ◯ ___ ___ ___ ◯◯ courts

and from house to ◯◯◯ ___ ___ , they

___ ___ ◯◯ ___ stopped ___ ◯ ___ ___ ___ ___ ___ ___

and proclaiming the ___ ___ ___ ◯   ___ ___ ___ ◯ that

◯ ___ ◯ ___ ___ is the Christ. (Acts 5:42)

Why were the disciples brave? T ___ ___ ___   L ___ ___ ___ ___

J ___ ___ ___ ___.

Stones of Death
and Goads to Life

Introduction

[Jesus said,] "Be faithful, even to the point of death, and I will give you the crown of life."

Revelation 2:10

A LITTLE group of people huddled together in a dimly lit room. They talked in low voices in their underground church. "I heard the authorities are searching every house to see if they can discover any Christian churches. Maybe we should not try to meet together anymore," said one man.

"But I need these few minutes with Christian friends to read the Bible and talk about Jesus," said another. "I'm willing to take a chance that we won't be discovered. Let's pray and ask God to keep us safe."

"Yes, let's do that," said an old lady. "But this may cost us our lives. We all know that some people in our country have been put in jail, and some have been killed for their faith."

A child spoke up then: "I love Jesus. Let's sing a song and think about him."

Very softly, they all began to sing, "Jesus loves me, this I know. . . ."

Suddenly, there was a pounding on the door. *Was that the authorities, come to put them in prison? Would they be killed?* No, it was another Christian who had come to join them. The brave Christians held hands and prayed.

An "underground church" is a group of Christians who must meet together in secret because the leaders of their country do not accept Christianity. Churches like that exist in some countries today.

Many Christians have been martyred through the centuries because of their faith. In fact, more Christians were killed for their faith in the 20th century than in all other centuries combined.

The Bible tells about the first Christian martyr.

The Facts, Please!

1. *Stoning.* People who broke certain laws in ancient Israel were stoned to death. Two witnesses testified against a criminal; then men hurled stones at him until he was dead.
2. *Goad.* This was a stick, eight to nine feet long. Its end was tipped with a sharp iron point. If oxen didn't want to move or were too slow, a farmer prodded them with a goad. Some oxen kicked against the goad, but this did them no good.

3. *Gentiles.* Any person who is not Jewish is a Gentile.
At first the disciples thought the gospel was for Jews
only. They learned this was wrong. Jesus told them to
go into all the world and preach to every person.

Bible Story: A Persecutor Gets Persecuted
Acts 6:8-15; 7:51—8:3; 9:1-19; 26:1-23; 2 Timothy 4:7-8

My name is Paul. From the time I was a child, I
tried to obey all the Jewish laws. I studied under a great
teacher of the Law and was a strict Pharisee. I did not believe
Jesus was God's Son.

I felt I pleased God when I persecuted those who did
believe in Jesus. I put Christians in prison and agreed to
their death.

One day I was present at the trial of a Christian named
Stephen. He preached a long sermon to us. He said the
Jewish leaders had betrayed and murdered God's Son. Oh,
how angry we were!

Stephen said, "I see heaven open and the Son of Man
standing at the right hand of God." I watched as the people
covered their ears. Yelling as loudly as they could, they
dragged Stephen out of the city. There, I gave some of the
Jewish leaders my approval to stone Stephen to death.

After that, I went from house to house, dragging Christians off to prison. Many were killed. One day I headed for
Damascus with some other men. We planned to take Christians from that city to the prison in Jerusalem.

Suddenly, a light from heaven, brighter than the sun, shone around me. As I fell to the ground, I heard a voice asking me why I was persecuting him. He said, "It is hard for you to kick against the goads." I knew what he meant. I had been fighting against a voice inside that told me I was doing wrong.

I asked, "Who are you, Lord?"

"I am Jesus, whom you are persecuting," the Lord said. "Get up now. I am sending you as a witness for me." Jesus! He really is God's Son! Right then, I believed in him as my Savior and Lord. Soon I began telling others about him.

I have preached for many years now—first to the Jewish people and then to the Gentiles. I, the persecutor, now bear on my own body the scars of many persecutions for the sake of Jesus, my Savior. I have fought the good fight. I have finished my race. I have kept the faith. Now a crown awaits me in heaven.

This Is for You

Paul was the first missionary to the Gentiles. He wrote 13 New Testament books and may have written the book of Hebrews also. Paul suffered many persecutions for preaching the gospel. Historians say the wicked Roman emperor Nero had Paul beheaded for his faith. If that's true, Paul, too, was a martyr for Jesus' sake.

What would Paul tell you about being faithful to Jesus if you could talk to Paul today? He would tell you the same thing he told young Timothy in a letter from his jail cell: "Endure hardship with us like a good soldier of Christ Jesus" (2 Timothy 2:3).

What do you do when it's hard to live as Jesus wants you to live? Do you keep on being faithful, even when you're the only one doing so? Are you a good soldier of the cross?

Right now Christians are being persecuted in many countries. Even children are suffering for Jesus' sake. Don't forget to pray for them every day. If you learn of ways you can send help to them, be sure to do it.

Fill in the Blanks:
The Sufferings of Paul

Open your Bible to 2 Corinthians 11:24-27. Use words from these verses to fill in the blanks.

Some ways in which Paul suffered:

Five times he received 39 _____ with whips. Three times

he was beaten with _____. Once he was _____.

Three times he was _____. He was in danger from

_____ , _____ , his _____ , and the

_____. He was in danger in the _____ ,

the _____ , and at _____. As he labored and

toiled, he often went without _____. He knew

_____ and _____ and often had no _____.

He had been_____ and _____.

A Race, a Judge, a Gift, and Rewards

Introduction

Watch out, so that you do not lose the prize for which we have been working so hard. Be diligent so that you will receive your full reward.

2 John 1:8 (NLT)

SUGIA lived at a mission school in India. She came from a poor family that could not take care of her. One day Sugia received Jesus as her Savior. After that, she dreamed about seeing Jesus in heaven. She wanted to stay at the school, but Jesus told her to teach other children about him.

"Each person you win to me will be like a jewel in your crown in heaven," Sugia heard Jesus say. She wondered how she could win anyone. All the children at the school were already saved.

One day Sugia won first prize in a Bible memory contest.

The prize was two rupees (about one dollar). "I'm rich!" Sugia said. "I have never had any jewelry. Now I can buy some beads!"

Then she remembered there were some children who lived in the village near the school. They had never heard of Jesus. She could buy some little Bible picture books for the missionaries to give them.

"I'll keep one rupee for myself and give one to buy books," Sugia decided. Still, she wasn't satisfied. The next day the missionary received a little packet with Sugia's whole prize. Finally she had a chance to win someone to Jesus, and that's what she wanted to do more than anything else. She knew that someday she would live with Jesus in heaven. She could wait to get her jewels then!

THE FACTS, PLEASE!

1. *Foot racing.* The first athletic event in the ancient Olympic games was the foot race. The games go farther back than history records, but the official list of winners began in 776 B.C. The games were well known in New Testament times. Contestants trained under strict rules. When a race ended, a herald proclaimed the name of the winner and his city. Then the winner received a wreath made from the leaves of an olive tree.
2. *Judgment seat of Christ.* This is not a judgment to decide if we go to heaven or hell. It is a place set up in heaven, where only believers will be. It is not a judgment of our sins. It is where Jesus gives us rewards for the work we have done for him.

3. *Gifts and rewards.* Salvation is a gift that we can't earn. Jesus paid for it when he died on the cross. We accept the gift by receiving Jesus as Savior. We can't earn salvation, we *can* earn rewards by faithfully doing good work for Jesus.

Bible Story: Rewards at the End of the Race
1 Corinthians 3:10-15; 9:24-27; Philippians 3:13-14; Hebrews 12:1-2

Ready, get set, go! Living the Christian life is like running a race. Paul said, "Run in such a way as to get the prize. Everyone who competes in the games goes into strict training. They do it to get a crown that will not last; but we do it to get a crown that will last forever."

At the end of the Christian race, every runner will receive rewards. Some Christians will get far more than others will. We will get our rewards for the work we do for Jesus. This will happen when he comes again someday to take us to heaven. There he will sit on his judgment seat and judge us for our works.

What are works? They are the things we do to serve Jesus. Some examples are: giving money to church and missions, being kind and helpful to a neighbor, taking the time to practice singing in a church choir, and telling others about Jesus.

The judgment will be like a fire that burns up the bad and leaves the good. The works we have done to please ourselves will be like wood, hay, and straw. They will burn up. The works we have done to please Jesus will be like gold, silver, and costly jewels. They won't burn. We will get rewards for them. They will show how much we loved Jesus in this life.

Our reward will include a crown. The Olympic runners received crowns that would wither. If we follow the rules of our race as Christians, we can receive a crown that lasts forever.

This Is For You

Jesus wants us to receive all the rewards he has for us. He will not overlook anything we do for him. Even giving a cup of cold water to a thirsty person can earn a reward. Jesus warns us not to lose any of our rewards by being unfaithful.

Losing rewards could make us ashamed. That is especially true because of what we will do with our crowns. Revelation 4:10-11 tells about laying crowns before Jesus' feet and saying, "You are worthy, our Lord and God, to receive glory and honor and power." What a wonderful way to worship Jesus!

Some Christians will have only a few rewards to lay at Jesus' feet. When they see the nail scars in his hands and feet, they will understand how much Jesus did for them. Then how will they feel?

Are you faithfully running your race of life? How much will you have to place in front of your Savior? Will Jesus look at you and say, "Well done, good and faithful servant" (Matthew 25:21)? It's not too late to begin earning your rewards!

Cross Out Letters:
How to Run the Race

To correctly fill in the blanks in the verse, first cross out the letters *B*, *Q*, and *Z*. Then write the remaining letters in order from left to right.

B B L E Z T U Z Q S QT B B H R Z QB O WB O Q F F B E V Q

E Z R Y T B H Z Z I NG Z QT H B A B T H Z I B N D Q B E R

S A N B D T H B B E Q S I N Z T B H Q A T S B O E A Q S B B

I L Z Z Y E N Q T B A N Z G L QE S A N D B Q L Z E T U Q S

R U B N W Z I QT H P B E R Q S Z E V E R A N Z C E B T H Q

E R B B A C Q E Z MB A R Q K B B E D B OUT F O Z R U B S

—— —— —— —— —— ——— —— ——— ——— ———

—— ——— ——— —— —— ——— —— ——— ——— ———

—— ——— ——— —— ——— —— ——— —— ——

—— ——— —— ——— —— ——— —— ——— ———

—— ——— ——— ———— , —— —— ——— ———

—— —— ——— —— ——— ———

—— ——— ——— —— ——— ——— —— —— ———

—— ——— —— ——— ——— —— ———

—— —— —— —— ——. (Hebrews 12:1)

Believers, Unbelievers, and Future Things

Introduction

How do you benefit if you gain the whole world but lose your own soul in the process? Is anything worth more than your soul?

Mark 8:36-37 (NLT)

A FEW years ago a man bought a picture at a flea market in Philadelphia for four dollars. When he came home, he took the picture out of its frame. To his great amazement he found underneath it a copy of the Constitution of the United States.

Appraisers examined the paper and found it was an original copy of the Constitution. It was printed on the night of

July 4, 1776. Later the man sold his four-dollar purchase for over two million dollars!

Imagine how the person must have felt who sold the valuable paper for only four dollars! He had not looked farther than the worthless picture on the outside.

Many people live just to enjoy a few pleasures today and are not concerned about their future. They disobey God and sell their souls to Satan for worthless bubbles that will soon burst. But eternity never ends. Shouldn't we think about where we will spend it?

THE FACTS, PLEASE!

1. *Believers.* People who believe in Jesus as their Savior.
2. *Unbelievers.* People who do not believe in Jesus as Savior.
3. *The Rapture.* The time when Jesus comes in the air and takes all believers to heaven.
4. *Heaven.* The eternal home of God, angels, and believers.
5. *Tribulation.* Great trouble on earth for seven years, beginning after the Rapture.
6. *Second Coming.* At the end of the tribulation, Jesus and all believers will come back to earth.
7. *Millennium.* The 1,000-year reign of Jesus on earth. It will be a time of peace and blessing.
8. *Great White Throne.* This follows the Millennium. It is the time when Jesus will judge all unbelievers who have ever lived. They will be sent to the lake of fire.
9. *Lake of fire.* This is another name for hell. It describes the final eternal home of Satan, demons, and unbelievers.

Bible Story: Millions Vanish from the Earth
1 Thessalonians 4:13-18; Revelation 20:11–22:7

It could happen any time. Believers will be going about their daily living. Suddenly, they will hear the loud shout of Jesus as he comes through the clouds. An angel's voice will speak, and a trumpet will blow loudly.

The believers who have died will come back to life, with their bodies made new. Living believers will get new bodies. Millions of them will leave the earth, meet the Lord in the air, and go with him to heaven. There, Jesus will give rewards to believers for faithful service. We will enjoy the wedding supper of Jesus, the Lamb.

While believers rejoice in heaven, unbelievers will be on earth for seven years of tribulation. They will endure the worst troubles, war, famine, and evil the world has ever known.

Then the Lord will return to earth, riding on a white horse. All believers will be with him. He will reign on earth for 1,000 years, and we will reign with him.

After this Jesus will judge sinners at the Great White Throne Judgment. All unbelievers from the beginning of time will be there. They will be sent to the lake of fire.

But believers will enjoy heaven forever! The city will be made of gold, as pure and shiny as clear glass. The foundation will be 12 layers of many different kinds of jewels, making it look like a rainbow. The huge wall around the city will be as clear as crystal.

There will be no sorrow, sickness, or sin in heaven. We will need no sun. God, with all his glory, will be the light. We can be with Jesus and with all of our Christian family members and friends. Forever we will be happy, serving God and enjoying our beautiful, perfect home.

This Is for You

The Lamb's Book of Life is a most important book. Your name must be there in order to be in heaven. How do you get it there? Believe on Jesus as your Savior and Lord. Don't put this off! Remember, Jesus can come at any time. He will not give you any advance notice.

Do you see why it is so important to plan for eternity? It may seem like a long time from now. And it might be, but no one knows that. Jesus could come this very day. Then you would have no more opportunity to be saved from your sins.

If you are a believer, are you living to please yourself or Jesus? When he comes back, there will be no more time to serve him and earn rewards.

Don't just look at the closeup picture and do wrong things that seem like fun. What good is it if you gain the whole world but lose your soul? Think about what is beyond the present. Get ready for eternity. Let's meet in heaven, OK? *See the last page of this book.*

Match-Up:
Believers and Unbelievers

Draw lines from *believers* and from *unbelievers* to the words that apply to them.

1. will be at the wedding supper of the Lamb.

2. have never believed in Jesus as Savior.

Believers

3. will go up to meet Jesus in the air.

4. will receive rewards in heaven for serving God.

5. will be in the lake of fire forever.

Unbelievers

6. will not find their names in the Book of Life.

7. will enjoy heaven forever.

8. will reign with Jesus in the Millennium.

9. will have great trouble in the Tribulation.

10. have believed in Jesus as Savior.

Answers

Devotion 1

```
W  P  L  E  H  S  A  T  A  N  U  Y  T
R  T  N  A  W  H  Y  W  I  S  E  N  R
S  S  G  O  D  L  B  E  L  I  E  V  E
K  G  P  O  I  S  O  N  O  U  S  E  E
N  E  N  M  O  T  A  D  A  M  N  D  S
O  L  A  C  F  D  A  V  B  T  S  I  N
W  F  K  R  R  A  E  T  I  E  E  L  E
L  T  E  A  U  V  E  C  P  O  L  G  A
E  S  D  W  I  D  I  E  D  M  R  L  K
D  T  O  L  T  N  G  A  R  D  E  N  Y
G  F  O  R  G  I  V  E  D  E  N  T  N
E  D  F  C  C  R  O  S  S  N  A  K  E
```

Devotion 2

In LAMBS	but not in	SLAM	B
In SLAW	but not in	WAS	L
In NOTE	but not in	TEN	O
In BOAT	but not in	TAB	O
In CRADLE	but not in	CLEAR	D

Reading down, what word have you written on the lines above? _Blood_

1. "Without the shedding of __BLOOD__ there is no

_F O R G I V E N E S S_ ." (Hebrews 9:22)
c-1 b-2 a-4 b-1 a-1 c-4 c-2 c-3 c-2 a-2 a-2

2. "To him who loves us and has __F R E E D__ us from
c-1 a-4 c-2 c-2 a-3

our sins by his __BLOOD__ ." (Revelation 1:5)

3. "The __BLOOD__ of Jesus, his Son,

_P U R I F I E S_ us from all sin." (1 John 1:7)
b-3 b-4 a-4 a-1 c-1 a-1 c-2 a-2

Devotion 3

1. God promised Abraham an

I N H E R I T A N C E in the place
H M G D Q H S Z M B D

where he was going.

2. Abraham O B E Y E D God and went, making his
N A D X D C

home in the promised land by F A I T H .
E Z H S G

3. Abraham L I V E D in T E N T S
K H U D C S D M S R

300

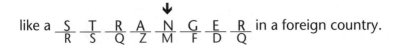

like a <u>S</u> <u>T</u> <u>R</u> <u>A</u> <u>N</u> <u>G</u> <u>E</u> <u>R</u> in a foreign country.
   R   S   Q   Z   M   F   D   Q

Abraham looked forward to going to **heaven**. Read Hebrews 11:8-10.

Devotion 4

1. Joseph's father gave him a coat of many — colors.
2. Joseph's brothers were — jealous.
3. They put him in a — cistern.
4. Then they sold him to some — merchants.
5. Joseph ended up in Egypt as a — slave.
6. Potiphar's wife lied about Joseph to her — husband.
7. Potiphar put Joseph in — prison.
8. People always found Joseph could be — trusted.
9. Joseph told Pharaoh the meaning of his — dreams.
10. Joseph advised Pharaoh about the coming — famine.
11. Pharaoh made Joseph an important — ruler.
12. Joseph saved many people from — starving.
13. Joseph's family all moved to — Egypt.
14. God worked all things in Joseph's life for — good.

Devotion 5

"<u>T</u> <u>H</u> <u>E</u> <u>L</u> <u>O</u> <u>R</u> <u>D</u> <u>I</u> <u>S</u> <u>N</u> <u>O</u> <u>T</u>
10 17 13 14 12 16 11 15 9 8 12 10

<u>S</u> <u>L</u> <u>O</u> <u>W</u> <u>I</u> <u>N</u> <u>K</u> <u>E</u> <u>E</u> <u>P</u> <u>I</u> <u>N</u> <u>G</u>
9 14 12 7 15 8 6 13 13 5 15 8 4

$$\frac{H}{17} \ \frac{I}{15} \ \frac{S}{9} \quad \frac{P}{5} \ \frac{R}{16} \ \frac{O}{12} \ \frac{M}{1} \ \frac{I}{15} \ \frac{S}{9} \ \frac{E}{13}, \quad \frac{A}{18} \ \frac{S}{9}$$

$$\frac{S}{9} \ \frac{O}{12} \ \frac{M}{1} \ \frac{E}{13} \quad \frac{U}{2} \ \frac{N}{8} \ \frac{D}{11} \ \frac{E}{13} \ \frac{R}{16} \ \frac{S}{9} \ \frac{T}{10} \ \frac{A}{18} \ \frac{N}{8} \ \frac{D}{11}$$

$$\frac{S}{9} \ \frac{L}{14} \ \frac{O}{12} \ \frac{W}{7} \ \frac{N}{8} \ \frac{E}{13} \ \frac{S}{9} \ \frac{S}{9} .\text{" 2 Peter 3:9}$$

Why do we think God is slow? Because we don't

  UNDERSTAND   **time the way he does.**

Devotion 6

```
P R O V E G L O R Y G
R M S T A R V E I Q O
O I A W I U C L O U D
V L B O W M A N N A P
I L B H O B M G M I O
D I A E R L P A E L T
E O T A M E A T F F F
D N H V S D M H I E O
D E S E R T E E R D O
D E W N M E B R E A D
```

1. God will give M E what he knows is best for M E .
2. I will try not to complain.
3. I will thank God for what he gives M E .

Devotion 7

↓

1. Carry your <u>B</u> <u>I</u> <u>B</u> <u>L</u> <u>E</u> to school.
    A H A K D

2. <u>A</u> <u>D</u> <u>M</u> <u>I</u> <u>T</u> you are a Christian.
    Z C L H S

3. <u>A</u> <u>T</u> <u>T</u> <u>E</u> <u>N</u> <u>D</u> church faithfully.
    Z S S D M C

4. Say <u>N</u> <u>O</u> to sinful actions.
    M N

5. <u>O</u> <u>B</u> <u>E</u> <u>Y</u> God in all things.
    N A D X

6. <u>P</u> <u>R</u> <u>A</u> <u>Y</u> before you eat.
    O Q Z X

7. Gladly <u>S</u> <u>E</u> <u>R</u> <u>V</u> <u>E</u> God and others.
    R D Q U D

**If you do these things, you will be flying <u>BANNERS</u>
to honor God.**

Devotion 8

"'<u>L O V E</u>   <u>T H E</u>   <u>L O R D</u>   <u>Y O U R</u>   <u>G O D</u>

W<u>I T H</u>   A<u>L L</u>   Y<u>O U R</u>   <u>H E A R T</u>   AND

W<u>I T H</u>   A<u>L L</u>   Y<u>O U R</u>   S<u>O U L</u>   AND

W<u>I T H</u>   A<u>L L</u>   Y<u>O U R</u>   S<u>T R E N G T H</u>

AND   W<u>I T H</u>   A<u>L L</u>   Y<u>O U R</u>   M<u>I N D</u>'; AND

'<u>L O V E</u>   Y<u>O U R</u>   N<u>E I G H B O R</u>   <u>A S</u>

Y<u>O U R S E L F</u>.'" (Luke 10:27)

Devotion 9

NEVER (SOMEDAY) TOMORROW

Devotion 10

T	X	U	R	C	Z	N	H	F	R	J	O
X	M	E	Z	H	J	V	I	X	C	H	L
A	Z	J	N	D	H	C	D	X	O	Z	G
O	G	H	O	H	X	Z	D	W	H	J	C

"T U R N   F R O M   E V I L

A N D   D O   G O O D." (Psalm 34:14)

Devotion 11

1. _J_ _E_ _S_ _U_ _S_ never sinned, so he is _H_ _O_ _L_ _Y_.
   1-6 3-5 2-7 3-7 2-7   1-5 2-6 1-7 3-4

2. All people are _G_ _U_ _I_ _L_ _T_ _Y_ of sin.
                  2-5 3-7 2-4 1-7 1-4 3-4

3. _J_ _E_ _S_ _U_ _S_   _B_ _O_ _R_ _E_ our sins in his body on
   1-6 3-5 2-7 3-7 2-7   1-8 2-6 3-6 3-5

the _C_ _R_ _O_ _S_ _S_ as if he were _G_ _U_ _I_ _L_ _T_ _Y_ .
    3-8 3-6 2-6 2-7 2-7   2-5 3-7 2-4 1-7 1-4 3-4

4. If we _B_ _E_ _L_ _I_ _E_ _V_ _E_ in _J_ _E_ _S_ _U_ _S_ ,
         1-8 3-5 1-7 2-4 3-5 2-8 3-5   1-6 3-5 2-7 3-7 2-7

he will forgive our sins and wash them away.

5. Then he makes us _H_ _O_ _L_ _Y_ in his sight.
                    1-5 2-6 1-7 3-4

6. Those who don't _B_ _E_ _L_ _I_ _E_ _V_ _E_ in
                   1-8 3-5 1-7 2-4 3-5 2-8 3-5

_J_ _E_ _S_ _U_ _S_ will be _G_ _U_ _I_ _L_ _T_ _Y_
1-6 3-5 2-7 3-7 2-7   2-5 3-7 2-4 1-7 1-4 3-4
of their sins forever.

Devotion 12

~~road~~ Do not ~~road~~ ~~army~~ be ~~giant~~
~~army~~ afraid ~~king~~ land of ~~sword~~ ~~king~~
~~giant~~ them ~~land~~ ~~road~~ the ~~giant~~ Lord
~~king~~ your ~~land~~ God ~~sword~~ himself will
fight ~~army~~ ~~sword~~ for ~~giant~~ ~~king~~ you

" <u>Do</u>   <u>not</u>   <u>be</u>   <u>afraid</u> <u>of</u>   <u>them</u> ;

<u>the</u>   <u>Lord</u>   <u>your</u>   <u>God</u>   <u>himself</u>   <u>will</u>

<u>fight</u>   <u>for</u>   <u>you</u> ." (Deuteronomy 3:22)

Devotion 13

" <u>I</u>   <u>H A V E</u>   <u>S E T</u>   <u>B E F O R E</u>
  H   G Z U D   R D S   A D E N Q D

<u>Y O U</u>   <u>L I F E</u>   <u>A N D</u>
X N T   K H E D   Z M C

<u>D E A T H</u>,   <u>B L E S S I N G S</u>
C D Z S G   A K D R R H M F R

<u>A N D</u>   <u>C U R S E S</u>.   <u>N O W</u>
Z M C   B T Q R D R   M N V

<u>C H O O S E</u>   <u>L I F E</u>,   <u>S O</u>
B G N N R D   K H E D   R N

<u>T H A T</u>   <u>Y O U</u>   <u>A N D</u>   <u>Y O U R</u>
S G Z S   X N T   Z M C   X N T Q

<u>C</u> <u>H</u> <u>I</u> <u>L</u> <u>D</u> <u>R</u> <u>E</u> <u>N</u>   <u>M</u> <u>A</u> <u>Y</u>
B G H K C Q D M   L Z X

<u>L</u> <u>I</u> <u>V</u> <u>E</u> ." Deuteronomy 30:19
K H U D

Devotion 14

1. The Midianites had an army of   32,000

2. Gideon started out with an army of   300

3. The number of fearful ones was   swords

4. The number of those who drank water on their
   knees was   trumpets

5. The number who lapped water was   22,000

6. The Midianites had weapons, including   135,000

7. Gideon and his men carried torches and   9,700

Gideon and his men <u>courageously</u> <u>trusted</u>

and <u>obeyed</u> <u>God</u> .

Devotion 15

<u>H</u> <u>I</u> <u>D</u> <u>E</u> God's Word in your heart (Psalm 119:11).

<u>P</u> <u>R</u> <u>A</u> <u>Y</u> continually (1 Thessalonians 5:17).

Go regularly to the <u>H</u> <u>O</u> <u>U</u> <u>S</u> <u>E</u> of God (Psalm 122:1).

<u>A</u> <u>V</u> <u>O</u> <u>I</u> <u>D</u> every kind of evil (1 Thessalonians 5:22).

Do not F O (L) L O W the crowd to do wrong
(Exodus 23:2).

O F F E (R) your body to God as a living sacrifice
(Romans 12:1).

Let your L I G H (T) shine before men (Matthew 5:16).

Write the letters inside the circles here:

H I P Y S O I L R T

Answer: The H O L Y   S P I R I T .

Devotion 16

1. _S_ "No, you can't have any of my candy. I want it all."
2. _J_ "I know you're tired, Mom. I'll wash the dishes."
3. _J_ "I won't go swimming. It's Sunday, and I'm going to church."
4. _S_ "Let's play ball instead of going to choir practice."
5. _S_ "Wait till you hear this gossip about Mike."
6. _J_ "I'll read the Bible first; then I'll play outside."
7. _S_ "Let's put these toys in our pockets. The clerk will never see us."
8. _J_ "I won't do that, because Jesus would never do it."
9. _J_ "I'll see you at the pole for prayer tomorrow."
10. _S_ "I'll tell Dad a little white lie to keep from getting punished."

DEVOTION 17

S	T	R	O	N	G	H	O	L	D
1	2	3	4	5	6	7	8	9	10

DEVOTION 18

<u>i</u> <u>m</u> <u>m</u> <u>e</u> <u>a</u> <u>s</u> <u>u</u> <u>r</u> <u>a</u> <u>b</u> <u>l</u> <u>y</u>
B-1 A-2 A-2 C-3 A-5 D-1 A-3 B-2 A-5 D-4 A-4 B-4

<u>m</u> <u>o</u> <u>r</u> <u>e</u>   <u>t</u> <u>h</u> <u>a</u> <u>n</u>   <u>a</u> <u>l</u> <u>l</u>
A-2 B-3 B-2 C-3   B-5 C-1 A-5 C-2   A-5 A-4 A-4

<u>w</u> <u>e</u>   <u>a</u> <u>s</u> <u>k</u>   <u>o</u> <u>r</u>   <u>i</u> <u>m</u> <u>a</u> <u>g</u> <u>i</u> <u>n</u> <u>e</u>,
D-2 C-3   A-5 D-1 C-4   B-3 B-2   B-1 A-2 A-5 D-3 B-1 C-2 C-3

<u>a</u> <u>c</u> <u>c</u> <u>o</u> <u>r</u> <u>d</u> <u>i</u> <u>n</u> <u>g</u>   <u>t</u> <u>o</u>   <u>h</u> <u>i</u> <u>s</u>
A-5 D-5 D-5 B-3 B-2   B-1 C-2 D-3   B-5 B-3   C-1 B-1 D-1

<u>p</u> <u>o</u> <u>w</u> <u>e</u> <u>r</u> that is at work within us. (Ephesians 3:20)
A-1 B-3 D-2 C-3 B-2

DEVOTION 19

Devotion 20

Therefore God exalted him to the highest place and

G	A	V	E		H	I	M	the	N	A	M	E
F	Z	U	D		G	H	L		M	Z	L	D

that is

A	B	O	V	E	every	N	A	M	E	,
Z	A	N	U	D		M	Z	L	D	

that at the

N	A	M	E	of	J	E	S	U	S
M	Z	L	D		I	D	R	T	R

every

K	N	E	E	should	B	O	W	, in
J	M	D	D		A	N	V	

H	E	A	V	E	N	and on	E	A	R	T	H
G	D	Z	U	D	M		D	Z	Q	S	G

and under the

E	A	R	T	H	, and every
D	Z	Q	S	G	

T	O	N	G	U	E		C	O	N	F	E	S	S
S	N	M	F	T	D		B	N	M	E	D	R	R

that

J	E	S	U	S		C	H	R	I	S	T	is
I	D	R	T	R		B	G	Q	H	R	S	

L	O	R	D	, to the glory of	G	O	D	the
K	N	Q	C		F	N	C	

F	A	T	H	E	R	(Philippians 2:9-11).
E	Z	S	G	D	Q	

DEVOTION 21

A L L - P O W E R F U L
A L L - P R E S E N T
A L L - K N O W I N G
U N C H A N G E A B L E
L O V E

S P I R I T (invisible, having no body)
T S R I I P

E T E R N A L (living forever; everlasting)
L E E R T A N

H O L Y (separate from sin; sacred)
Y H O L

R I G H T E O U S (being and doing right)
E R U O S H I G T

T R U T H (the absence of lies)
U T T H R

DEVOTION 22

The king's name was ____AHAB____ (8 down). The king wanted another man's __VINEYARD__ (2 down). The vineyardist was __NABOTH__ (9 across). The king's wife was named ____JEZEBEL____ (3 down). The king's wife had the vineyardist __STONED__ (5 down) to death. The prophet who came to the king was ____ELIJAH____ (6 across). He said the dogs would lick the king's __BLOOD__ (10 across). The tenth commandment is, "You shall not _COVET_ " (7 across).

Devotion 23

↓

"<u>G</u> <u>O</u> <u>D</u> so

<u>L</u> <u>O</u> <u>V</u> <u>E</u> <u>D</u> the world that he gave his one

and only <u>S</u> <u>O</u> <u>N</u> , that whoever believes in him

shall not <u>P</u> <u>E</u> <u>R</u> <u>I</u> <u>S</u> <u>H</u> but have

<u>E</u> <u>T</u> <u>E</u> <u>R</u> <u>N</u> <u>A</u> <u>L</u>

<u>L</u> <u>I</u> <u>F</u> <u>E</u> " (John 3:16).

The <u>G</u> <u>O</u> <u>S</u> <u>P</u> <u>E</u> <u>L</u> is the good news of salvation.

DEVOTION 24

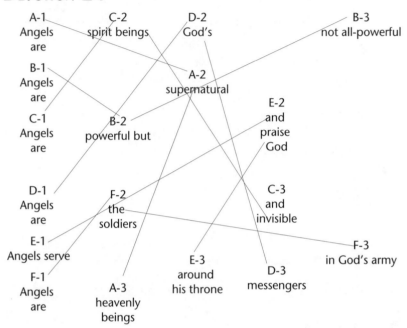

A-1
Angels are

C-2
spirit beings

D-2
God's

B-3
not all-powerful

B-1
Angels are

A-2
supernatural

C-1
Angels are

B-2
powerful but

E-2
and praise God

D-1
Angels are

F-2
the soldiers

C-3
and invisible

E-1
Angels serve

F-3
in God's army

F-1
Angels are

A-3
heavenly beings

E-3
around his throne

D-3
messengers

DEVOTION 25

God does not want us to be:

P R O U D (DROUP), B O A S T F U L
(ASTFULOB), H A U G H T Y (HATYHUG), or
M E A N (NAME).

God does want us to be:
      UBLHME   H U M B L E.

Devotion 26

H S T A E W D N D R T T U A E N

F Z A I L W S G A H J Y T H F O

P R S W O W C M A Y T L I H L F

E O K L W S O H C R I A D M

1. Jonah told the sailors that God had caused the storm because

Jonah H A D   R U N   A W A Y

F R O M   T H E   L O R D .

2. When Jonah sank into the sea, God S E N T   A

F I S H   T O   S W A L L O W

H I M .

Devotion 27

"W H O M   S H A L L   I   S E N D ,
 5 15 11 9   6 15 2 17 17   14   6 12 8 18

A N D   W H O   W I L L   G O
 2 8 18   5 15 11   5 14 17 17   3 11

F O R   U S ?"
16 11 13   6

"W H A T   S H A L L   I   S A Y ,
 5 15 2 10   6 15 2 17 17   14   6 2 7

315

L O R D ,   T O   T H E E ?
17 11 13 18   10 11   10 15 12 12

T H E   H A R V E S T   I S
10 15 12   15 2 13 4 12 6 10   14 6

G R E A T ,   T H E   W O R K E R S
3 13 12 2 10   10 15 12   5 11 13 1 12 13 6

N O T   M A N Y ,   L O R D , H E R E
8 11 10   9 2 8 7   17 11 13 18 15 12 13 12

A M   I ,   S E N D   M E ."
2 9   14   6 12 8 18   9 12

Devotion 28

"I am the Lord, your God, who takes hold of your right hand and
and says to you, Do not fear; I WILL HELP YOU ." (Isaiah 41:13).

I S A I A H

W A L L

S I E G E

L O R D

B A T T L E S

H E Z E K I A H

S E N N A C H E R I B

I N S U L T

T E M P L E

P R A Y E R S

O F F I C E R S

H U G E

Devotion 29

```
T O N O D O W R
F D N T O C R I
O L H T H E C L
T L O W W C F L
N O L W O R O W
G F [J E S U S] D
I D W R O D N I
R W G N I O I N
T R W R O N G G
```

We should follow **J E S U S** in doing right.

Devotion 30

"B_e_ f_a_ _i_thf_u_l, _e_v_e_n t_o_ the p_o_ _i_nt
_o_f d_e_ _a_th, a_nd I w_i_ll g_i_v_e_ y_o_ _u_
th_e_ cr_o_wn _o_f l_i_f_e_." (Revelation 2:10)

Devotion 31

T O D O G O D'S W O R K ,
S N C N F N C R V N Q J

D O N'T E V E R Q U I T ,
C N M S D U D Q P T H S

K E E P   G O I N G   R I G H T
J D D O   F N H M F   Q H F G S

A L O N G ,   F O R   G O D   I S
Z K N M F   E N Q   F N C   H R

T H E R E   B E S I D E   Y O U ,
S G D Q D   A D R H C D   X N T

A N D   H E ' L L   H E L P   Y O U
Z M C   G D K K   G D K O   X N T

T O   B E   S T R O N G .
S N   A D   R S Q N M F

Devotion 32

↓

P R A Y , believing God will do what he promised.
10 11 1 15

R E A D the Bible to learn about God's promises.
11 4 1 3

O B E Y God in all things.
9 2 4 15

M E E T God's conditions for claiming his promises.
7 4 4 13

I N Jesus' name is always the way to pray.
6 8

S A Y , "God's will be done."
12 1 15

<u>E</u> <u>N</u> <u>D</u> <u>U</u> <u>R</u> <u>E</u> . Don't give up!
4   8   3 14 11 4

Be <u>S</u> <u>A</u> <u>T</u> <u>I</u> <u>S</u> <u>F</u> <u>I</u> <u>E</u> <u>D</u> with what God does
12 1 13 6 12 5 6 4 3

for you.

Remember, God always keeps his <u>P</u> <u>R</u> <u>O</u> <u>M</u> <u>I</u> <u>S</u> <u>E</u> <u>S</u>!

Devotion 33

Devotion 34

Set 1—What Bible characters gave

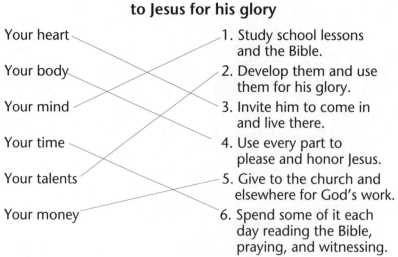

Angels

Mary

Shepherds

The Magi

1. worship, praise, and a witness about Jesus

2. messages about Jesus from God to people

3. her body, her love, and her prayers

4. worship and three special gifts

Set 2—How you can use these gifts to Jesus for his glory

Your heart

Your body

Your mind

Your time

Your talents

Your money

1. Study school lessons and the Bible.

2. Develop them and use them for his glory.

3. Invite him to come in and live there.

4. Use every part to please and honor Jesus.

5. Give to the church and elsewhere for God's work.

6. Spend some of it each day reading the Bible, praying, and witnessing.

Devotion 35

GOOD BEST TO ONLY GIVE ENOUGH MY IS JESUS
DOGO STEB OT LYNO IVEG GOUNEH YM SI SUEJS
  5   3   7   1   8   6   2   4   9

<u>ONLY</u>   <u>MY</u>   <u>BEST</u>   <u>IS</u>   <u>GOOD</u> <u>ENOUGH</u>
 1   2   3   4   5   6

<u>TO</u>   <u>GIVE</u>   <u>JESUS</u> .
 7   8   9

Devotion 36

A C D E F G H . . . . . . <u>B</u>   O P Q S T U V . . . . . . <u>R</u>

C D E F G H J . . . . . . <u>I</u>   J K L M O P Q . . . . . . <u>N</u>

D E F H I J K . . . . . . <u>G</u>   Q R S U V W X . . . . . . <u>T</u>

G I J K L M N . . . . . . <u>H</u>   B C D F G H I . . . . . . <u>E</u>

J K L N O P Q . . . . . . <u>M</u>   P Q R S U V W . . . . . . <u>T</u>

L M N P Q R S . . . . . . <u>O</u>   H I K L M N O . . . . . . <u>J</u>

A B C D F G H . . . . . . <u>E</u>   R T U V W X Y . . . . . . <u>S</u>

S T V W X Y Z . . . . . . <u>U</u>   O P Q R T U V . . . . . . <u>S</u>

The best help I can give my friends is to <u>B</u> <u>R</u> <u>I</u> <u>N</u> <u>G</u>

<u>T</u> <u>H</u> <u>E</u> <u>M</u>   <u>T</u> <u>O</u>   <u>J</u> <u>E</u> <u>S</u> <u>U</u> <u>S</u> .

Devotion 37

" S T O P J U D G I N G B Y
b-1 a-2 a-4 b-4   a-1 a-5 b-5 c-2 c-3 b-2 c-2   b-3 c-5

M E R E A P P E A R A N C E S ,
c-4 d-2 d-3 d-2 d-4 b-4 b-4 d-2 d-4 d-3 d-4 b-2 c-1 d-2 b-1

A N D M A K E A R I G H T
d-4 b-2 b-5 c-4 d-4 d-1 d-2 d-4 d-3 c-3 c-2 a-3 a-2

J U D G M E N T ." (John 7:24)
a-1 a-5 b-5 c-2 c-4 d-2 b-2 a-2

Devotion 38

	1	2	3	4	5	6	7	8	9	10
A	H	D	E	P	T	A	S	R	O	S
B	D	B	E	L	I	X	E	V	E	S
C	E	T	W	E	R	V	N	F	A	L
D	L	C	I	D	P	F	T	H	E	N
E	M	D	N	L	E	X	A	T	W	H
F	H	G	L	Y	I	Z	F	Q	R	E

"I tell you the truth, whoever __HEARS__ my word and
　　　　　　　　　　　　　　　　A

__BELIEVES__ him who sent me has __ETERNAL__
　　B　　　　　　　　　　　　　　　　　　C

__LIFE__ and will not be condemned; he has crossed
　D

over from __DEATH__ to __LIFE__ ." (John 5:24)
　　　　　　E　　　　　　F

Devotion 39

1. The man who helped the wounded man was the
   SAMARITAN .

2. This helper was a _NEIGHBOR_ to the hurt man.

3. A _LAWYER_ asked Jesus how to have eternal life.

4. A temple helper, a _LEVITE_ , passed by the hurt man.

5. We are to love _GOD_ with all our being.

6. The man who questioned Jesus called him "_TEACHER_."

7. _ROBBERS_ attacked the man, leaving him half dead.

8. The wounded man had been on his way to _JERICHO_ .

9. A _PRIEST_ was the first man to pass by the hurt man.

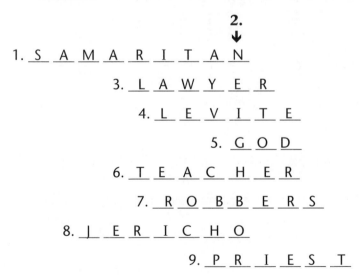

2.
↓
1. S A M A R I T A N

3. L A W Y E R

4. L E V I T E

5. G O D

6. T E A C H E R

7. R O B B E R S

8. J E R I C H O

9. P R I E S T

Devotion 40

2	8	5	3	3	6	3	5	9	6	8
+2	-2	-4	+4	+3	-4	+6	+5	-1	+7	+1
4	6	1	7	6	2	9	10	8	13	9
G	O	D	L	O	V	E	S	T	H	E

5	4	4	10	5	8	1	5	2	9	9
+2	+2	+6	-2	+6	-3	+0	+7	+7	-2	+5
7	6	10	8	11	5	1	12	9	7	14
L	O	S	T	A	N	D	W	E	L	C

4	6	12	7	5	10	6	2	5	2	7	6
+2	-3	-3	+3	+3	+3	+3	+1	+8	+4	-4	+3
6	3	9	10	8	13	9	3	13	6	3	9
O	M	E	S	T	H	E	M	H	O	M	E

GOD LOVES THE LOST
AND WELCOMES THEM
HOME.

Devotion 41

L	K	F	E	C	T	Q	E	V	M
J	E	R	C	Y	M	T	H	F	Q
I	N	K	F	G	T	C	F	H	A
T	M	Q	H	J	A	S	B	F	R
Q	E	C	F	K	A	T	M	H	P
J	R	A	M	I	C	S	J	E	T
H	K	E	C	L	M	O	F	R	D

L E T E V E R Y T H I N G

T H A T H A S B R E A T H

P R A I S E T H E L O R D .

(Psalm 150:6)

Does this include you? _Yes!_

Devotion 42

"No good _tree_ bears bad _fruit_ , nor does a bad _tree_ bear good _fruit_ . Each _tree_ is recognized by its own _fruit_ . People do not pick _figs_ from _thornbushes_ , or _grapes_ from _briers_ . The good _man_ brings good _things_ out of the good stored up in his _heart_ , and the evil _man_ brings evil _things_ out of the evil stored up in his _heart_ . For out of the overflow of his _heart_ his _mouth_ speaks." (Luke 6:43-45)

Devotion 43

Devotion 44

1. When Jesus died on the cross for our sins, he became our

<u>R</u> <u>E</u> <u>D</u> <u>E</u> <u>E</u> <u>M</u> <u>E</u> <u>R</u>.
 3   4   5   4   4   1   4   3

2. The robber who mocked Jesus was a

<u>R</u> <u>E</u> <u>J</u> <u>E</u> <u>C</u> <u>T</u> <u>E</u> <u>R</u> of the
 3   4   2   4   7 11 4   3

<u>R</u> <u>E</u> <u>D</u> <u>E</u> <u>E</u> <u>M</u> <u>E</u> <u>R</u>.
 3   4   5   4   4   1   4   3

3. The robber who believed in Jesus was a

<u>R</u> <u>E</u> <u>C</u> <u>E</u> <u>I</u> <u>V</u> <u>E</u> <u>R</u> of the
 3   4   7   4   8   9   4   3

<u>R</u> <u>E</u> <u>D</u> <u>E</u> <u>E</u> <u>M</u> <u>E</u> <u>R</u>.
 3   4   5   4   4   1   4   3

4. The <u>R</u> <u>E</u> <u>J</u> <u>E</u> <u>C</u> <u>T</u> <u>E</u> <u>R</u> went to <u>H</u> <u>E</u> <u>L</u> <u>L</u>.
       3   4   2   4   7 11 4   3   10 4   6   6

5. The <u>R</u> <u>E</u> <u>C</u> <u>E</u> <u>I</u> <u>V</u> <u>E</u> <u>R</u> went to
       3   4   7   4   8   9   4   3

<u>H</u> <u>E</u> <u>A</u> <u>V</u> <u>E</u> <u>N</u>.
10 4 12 9 4 13

Devotion 45

Verse	**Word**	↓
John 2:19	#14	t h r e e
Acts 3:15	#6	l i f e
Luke 24:39	#17	g h o s t
1 Corinthians 6:14	#10	d e a d
Acts 2:32	#3	r a i s e d
Psalm 49:15	#4	r e d e e m
Acts 1:3	#2	h i s
1 Corinthians 15:42	#15	s o w n
1 Corinthians 15:20	#4	i n d e e d
2 Corinthians 4:14	#3	k n o w

Devotion 46

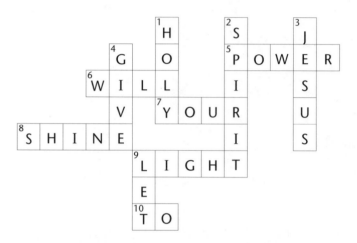

The __HOLY__ __SPIRIT__ __WILL__ __GIVE__
    (1 down) (2 down) (6 across) (4 down)

you __POWER__ __TO__ __LET__ __YOUR__
    (5 across) (10 across) (9 down) (7 across)

__LIGHT__ __SHINE__ for __JESUS__ .
(9 across)   (8 across)   (3 down)

Devotion 47

Day after d a y , in the t e m p l e courts
and from house to h o u s e , they
n e v e r stopped t e a c h i n g
and proclaiming the g o o d n e w s that
J e s u s is the Christ. (Acts 5:42)

Why were the disciples brave? T h e y L o v e d
J e s u s.

Devotion 48

Five times he received 39 __lashes__ with whips. Three times
he was beaten with ___rods___. Once he was ___stoned___.
Three times he was __shipwrecked__. He was in danger from
__rivers__ , __bandits__ , his __countrymen__ , and the
___Gentiles___. He was in danger in the ___city___ ,
the __country__ , and at __sea__. As he labored and
toiled, he often went without __sleep__. He knew
__hunger__ and __thirst__ and often had no __food__.
He had been __cold__ and __naked__.

Devotion 49

B B L E Z T U Z Q S Q T B B H R Z Q B O W B O Q F F B E V Q
E Z R Y T B H Z Z I N G Z Q T H B A B T H Z I B N D Q B E R
S A N B D T H B B E Q S I N Z T B H Q A T S B O E A Q S B B
I L Z Z Y E N Q T B A N Z G L Q E S A N D B Q L Z E T U Q S
R U B N W Z I Q T H P B E R Q S Z E V E R A N Z C E B T H Q
E R B B A C Q E Z M B A R Q K B B E D B O U T F O Z R U B S

L E T   U S   T H R O W   O F F
E V E R Y T H I N G   T H A T

H I N D E R S   A N D   T H E
S I N   T H A T   S O   E A S I L Y
E N T A N G L E S ,   A N D   L E T
U S   R U N   W I T H
P E R S E V E R A N C E   T H E
R A C E   M A R K E D   O U T
F O R   U S . (Hebrews 12:1)

Devotion 50

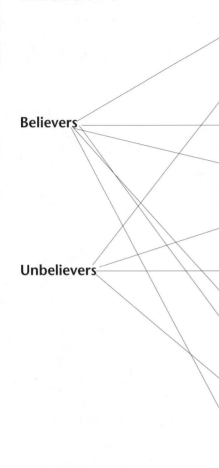

Believers

Unbelievers

1. will be at the wedding supper of the Lamb.

2. have never believed in Jesus as Savior.

3. will go up to meet Jesus in the air.

4. will receive rewards in heaven for serving God.

5. will be in the lake of fire forever.

6. will not find their names in the Book of Life.

7. will enjoy heaven forever.

8. will reign with Jesus in the Millennium.

9. will have great trouble in the Tribulation.

10. have believed in Jesus as Savior.

Bibliography

Sources most frequently used in researching the sections in this book titled "The Facts, Please!"

Child Evangelism Fellowship. *Children's Ministry Resource Bible.* Nashville, TN: Thomas Nelson Publishers, 1993.

Editorial Staff. *Funk and Wagnalls New Encyclopedia.* New York, NY: Funk and Wagnalls, Inc., 1993.

Editorial Staff. *Illustrated Dictionary of Bible Life and Times.* Pleasantville, NY: The Reader's Digest Association, 1997.

Editorial Staff. *World Book Encyclopedia.* Chicago, IL: Field Enterprises, Inc., 1995.

Gower, Ralph, and Fred H. Wight. *The New Manners and Customs of Bible Times.* Chicago, IL: Moody Press, 1987.

Keyes, Nelson Beecher. *Story of the Bible World.* Pleasantville, NY: The Reader's Digest Association, 1962.

Lockyer, Herbert, Sr., General Editor. *Nelson's Illustrated Bible Dictionary.* Nashville, TN: Thomas Nelson Publishers, 1986.

McElrath, William. *Bible Dictionary for Young Readers.* Nashville, TN: Broadman Press, 1965.

Price, Randall. *The Stones Cry Out.* Eugene, OR: Harvest House Publishers, 1997.

Schwartz, Max. *Machines, Buildings, Weaponry of Biblical Times.* Grand Rapids, MI: Fleming H. Revell Co., 1997.

Tenney, Merrill C. *The Zondervan Pictorial Bible Dictionary.* Grand Rapids, MI: Zondervan Publishing House, 1999.

Unger, Merrill F. *Unger's Bible Dictionary.* Chicago, IL: Moody Press, 1988.

Unger, Merrill F. *Unger's Commentary on the Old Testament*, Volumes 1 and 2. Chicago, IL: Moody Press, 1981.

Willmington, Harold L. *Willmington's Bible Handbook.* Wheaton, IL: Tyndale House Publishers, Inc., 1997.

Wilson, Etta. *Bible Encyclopedia: A First Reference Book.* Cincinnati, OH: Standard Publishing Co., 1995.

About the Author

Mary Rose Pearson accepted Jesus as her Savior when she was seven years old. More than 70 years later, there is nothing more important to her than helping other boys and girls receive Jesus, too.

Mary Rose is the author of over 20 books, as well as 600 short stories and devotions for children. For many years she wrote much of the material for the children's church sessions that she led.

In 1996 this author was named Writer of the Year by the Florida Christian Writers Conference. In 1999 she received the same award from American Christian Writers. Her Tyndale book *Frogs in Pharaoh's Bed,* to which this book is a companion, was on the C. S. Lewis Noteworthy List for 1995 and has sold more than 25,000 copies. She continues to submit many book proposals to publishers.

Mary Rose lives with her husband, retired evangelist M. N. Pearson, in Minneola, Florida, the town where she grew up. They have three children, twelve grandchildren, and five great-grandchildren!

The Good News of Salvation

Know It and Do It!

1. **Know it:** *All people have sinned.* "For all have sinned and fall short of the glory of God" (Romans 3:23). "If we confess our sins, he is faithful and just and will forgive us our sins" (1 John 1:9).

   Do it: *Admit you are a sinner and want to turn from your sin.* We were born sinners. We have all done things that do not please a holy God. Sin is doing bad things (like lying, stealing, disobeying, thinking bad thoughts, and saying bad words). Our sin separates us from God. But if we admit or confess our sin, it no longer separates us!

2. **Know it:** *God loves us and sent his Son to die for us.* "God demonstrates his own love for us in this: While we were still sinners, Christ died for us" (Romans 5:8). "He was raised on the third day according to the Scriptures" (1 Corinthians 15:4). "The Father has sent his Son to be the Savior of the world" (1 John 4:14).

   Do it: *Believe that Jesus died for your sins and rose again.* God loves us and sent his Son. Jesus never

337

sinned, but God put our sins on him when he was on the cross. Then Jesus came back to life. Believe it!

3. **Know it:** *You can choose whether or not to accept the gift of God's Son.* "To all who received him, to those who believed in his name, he gave the right to become children of God" (John 1:12). "Everyone who calls on the name of the Lord will be saved" (Romans 10:13). **Do it:** *Receive Jesus as your Savior and Lord.* God doesn't force us to accept the gift of salvation through his Son. But he patiently invites us because he loves us and wants us to be in his family. To accept God's gift of salvation, you can pray the prayer below.

Pray It and Then . . .

Pray it: Lord Jesus, I have sinned. I want to turn away from my sin. I believe you died for me and rose again. Please come into my heart and forgive my sins. Amen.

And then . . . After you ask Jesus to be your Savior, tell someone about it. Then be sure to read your Bible and talk to God each day. Every week you'll want to go to church, where you can learn more about Jesus and enjoy being with your new family—God's family!

IF YOU LIKED
Seven Ducks in Dirty Water,

CHECK OUT MARY ROSE PEARSON'S
Frogs in Pharaoh's Bed

ISBN 0-8423-1755-4